HONEY
ON THE
Sweet
POTATOES

The Letters and Legacy of
Leona Mae "Grandma" Moats

Joyce Harlukowicz

ISBN 978-1-68526-438-3 (Paperback)
ISBN 978-1-68526-439-0 (Digital)

Covenant Books
11661 Hwy 707
Murrells Inlet, SC 29576
www.covenantbooks.com

CONTENTS

ACKNOWLEDGEMENTS

The author extends grateful thanks to the Moats, Womack, Reid, and Wilson families for the source materials and anecdotal stories surrounding the life of Leona Mae "Grandma" Moats. Additional thanks are owed to Julie Cowles, who read every word of every draft of the story, a faithful and true editor and friend.

FOREWORD

This is a book about celebration.

This is a book about hope.

This is a book about how someone can impact your life just when you're not looking.

This is a book for fellow pilgrims in the Christian faith. I am taking you along on my journey of faith, a journey begun more than fifty years ago. I am making the pilgrimage common to all Christians learning to abide and live in communion with Christ and in obedience to his commands. This is work. Few, if any, Christians experience lives of ease, clarity, freedom from doubt, and freedom from the experience of suffering. There is perfect wisdom in the Apostle Paul's teaching in Philippians 2:12–13:

> Therefore, my beloved, as you have always obeyed, not as in my presence only, but now much more in my absence, work out your own salvation with fear and trembling; for it is God who works in you both to will and to do for His good pleasure. (NKJV)

For some of us, in God's providence, wisdom, and love, it is a solitary journey, at times on the margin of loneliness. But with a grateful heart in thankfulness and obedience to the One who saved me by grace through faith, I move forward. Works are the evidence of the faith within.

Working out our lives of faith: we are left to do that. It is *work*. It involves sacrifice, mistakes, and errors along with joys, comforts, and hope. God has given us everything we need to successfully navigate this labor: his Son, his Word, his Spirit, his church—composed of the worshiping community of which we are a part. In that worshiping community, we minister to one another, pray together over problems, lend an ear and solicit counsel, provide for one another's needs in real and tangible ways through service and sacrifice, share and celebrate answers to prayer. The pattern of God's design emerges: the collective wisdom of generations of the faithful whose examples are the signals and signposts by which we, if we're paying attention, can navigate the life of faith. Again, Paul in Philippians 3:17 urges us to observe, imitate, and emulate others who followed his example:

> Brethren, join in following my example, and note those who so walk, as you have us for a pattern. (Philippians 3:17 NKJV)

Following in the footsteps of those who love the Lord and are obedient to him encourages and energizes us:

> Let us hold fast the confession of our hope without wavering, for He who promised is faithful. And let us consider one another in order to stir up love and good works, not forsaking the assembling of ourselves together, as is the manner of some, but exhorting one another; and so much the more as you see the Day approaching. (Hebrews 10:23–25 NKJV)

Part of this journey I walked with Leona Mae "Grandma" Moats. By describing this gracious providential period in my life, let me make it perfectly clear: the focus of this book is on God, the glory of his mercy and grace, radiated and reflected by his servant Leona. She was one of those whom Paul well recommends we follow and emulate. How so?

Her story is that of a life well lived and through its illumination unfolds a salutary tale revealing the bonds of humanity in pursuit of apprehension of the Divine. She is humble and believed sincerely her life to be ordinary. She betrayed this assumption of "ordinary" through a dynamic and defining legacy—she was a writer. Leona was an avid reader in her youth. From this wellspring comes the desire to shape stories to be read by others. She wrote for the joy of expressing love for God and God's Word. She discovered the power of writing to bless other's lives, sharing things she learned through experience and reflection on the rocky paths of life. As closely as can be figured, she carried on these exquisite creative acts for more than sixty years. It is here our lives intersect: I, a lover of worthy stories, collecting them from a master storyteller, and thereby learning to live, work, and walk a life of faith.

This is a book for grandmothers. May this story become an encouragement for those who have reached the burnished time of an honored place in one's family, that of the bearer of wisdom, example, and grace. May you be inspired to persevere in faith, hope, and love, believing that the Lord will use your prudence, sometimes in ways unknowing, for the great benefit of your family for generations to come.

This is a book for grandchildren. The world around us is filled with false idols to whom it grants the delusions and gimmicks of sagacity, sophistication, and the allure of the urbane. Flee the attraction of the cosmopolitan, and seek worthy role models around you especially those who have lived and experienced a lot of life—they are as near as your very own family. And if not there, adopt them from another family. I can attest to the success of such an audacious adventure!

This is a book for those who doubt the faith. Seasons and times of testing and trouble are inevitable in our Christian lives. Our hearts are fortified and encouraged by the examples of others who have experienced and transcended the dark days of doubt, hardship, and fear. We find our own strength and confidence in the examples of God's faithful sustaining power in the lives of fellow heirs to salvation.

This is a book for those of steadfast faith. The history of the church is more than momentous and remarkable narratives of past events and people. The people and events surrounding us today serve to inspire us to persevere and affirm God's faithfulness. In this testimony, we should rejoice and celebrate! He who created the world and sustains all that is in it shall keep us to the end. Grandma Moats lived this truth in plain sight for all to see.

So I now turn the tables on Leona "Grandma" Moats and preserve her legacy, telling her story, often with her own words, and even with a few of mine.

PROLOGUE

I wait patiently in the gathering light of predawn. I remember the moment—one defined by the early, first unsteady notes of the robin, high in the boughs of the Norway spruces in the front yard, the branches a canopy over this old house, mine and the robin's. I wait for my ride; this is a passage I cannot make alone. The ride is quiet, uneventful, without conversation. A journey to the hospital seldom inspires convivial communion. I wish mightily to be back home in the presence of the robin's sweet morning opening.

The second-floor surgical waiting lounge at Beaumont Hospital is already alive with the gathering of those preparing for procedures. We find a cluster of chairs in a corner of the lounge, this small band of warriors assembled to enact the first assault on my unwelcomed diagnosis. Our circle includes our pastor, church members, friends; it will never include family members. My mother does not know. She will never know.

We prepare for prayer, hands joined, Pastor Jeff's long, gentle fingers completely engulfing my shaking palm. Daneen takes the left flank, her warm, strong grip impenetrable and defiant. But before the first chord of prayer can be struck, we stop—there is an unmistakable footfall approaching. We look up as Heidi, Pastor Jeff's wife, appears in tow with Leona "Grandma" Moats. Two elevator rides and a sprint all the way across the second-floor atrium leave her nearly breathless, but neither her eighty-four years nor chronic pulmonary fibrosis will prevent her presence in this moment, in this place. She stands behind me and lays her hands upon my shoulders like a mother bird's wings.

Now, we pray.

I met Grandma Moats a month before, at a Friday evening fellowship gathering at Pastor Jeff and Heidi Wilson's home. Grandma arrived to spend a few months with granddaughter Heidi and her family, part of a well-planned, loving decision to provide for Grandma's care. There are many stops on this schedule of hospitality composed of a daughter's and several granddaughters' homes; Florida, South Dakota, Nebraska, and Michigan travel mementoes adorn her suitcase. My first glimpse of this stranger to our gathering is like a lovely still life painting—Grandma in silhouette against a west window, the weak February evening light aglow on her perfectly grandmotherly hair, bent forward as her hands carve ham for our buffet meal. I have not the least idea that her hand, as in writing and authorship, would in time reveal her masterwork, a full-fledged concerto, a rhapsody filled with pages of meditations and musings on faith, family, and gratitude in a long-lived Christian life. For more than thirty-five years, Leona "Grandma" Moats carried on a letter-writing ministry sent to more than forty recipients each week. The letters arrive in the mailboxes of family and friends in her handwriting, one page, double-sided, hand-stamped and hand-addressed. I am added to the mailing list. The letters would from this time forward feed my spirit and soul.

CHAPTER 1

At the Kitchen Table

At the kitchen table in the cottage by the lake I sit, watching waves crash onshore from a blustery west wind. Though a sturdy desk and upright, equally sturdy chair in the study await my writing pursuits, the well-used old table here in the kitchen has a history. It reminds me of those who have come before us and leave their presence and their mark on our lives. I am still here, over ten years after the diagnosis; and more than ever, I am compelled to consider the gracious legacy of a humble Christian foremother whose example changed my life.

But I have much more than mere reminiscences in this recollection and revelation of the woman we affectionately call "Grandma," whom I shall reveal. She has become far more than a lovely family photograph to be collected and displayed reverently on a fireplace mantle. As I was brought into the rhythm and cadence of her life through her family, I discovered a life worth illuminating. Her life will speak to us spiritually and profoundly. Her great grace and legacy is the hope, stability, and comfort of a life founded on faith in Jesus Christ, prayer, and loving action.

Leona Mae Smith Moats was born in 1921 in Missouri Valley, Iowa. She and her sister, Ella Marie, were raised in the conservative heartland of our country, and she was shaped by the simple fundamental values of that robust and rugged era. She went to school; she did not graduate from high school. She worked jobs typical for young women: housekeeping and factory work. She married, raised children, joined and served her local church. She lived through the joys of family life and the sorrows of losing a child. Though living her married life first in Council Bluffs then in Honey Creek, Iowa, she and husband, Ronald, traveled in later years throughout the United States, her greatest joy visiting family in far-flung destinations. After the passing of her husband and when she was no longer able to live on her own in her home, she embarked on other journeys. She was cared for and resided with her daughter and granddaughters in turn as a loving and remarkably farsighted means to ensure well-being for an aging parent. It was on one of her sojourns with a granddaughter, who is a member of my church, where I became acquainted with Grandma—or perhaps I should say was drawn into her lustrous orbit.

However ordinary this seems, her life, as it turns out, is nothing ordinary, and its revelation is a powerful story and inspiration. The Lord placed Grandma in my life at a crucial intersection humanly and spiritually. I'd become accustomed to the solitary life, a career woman rising from an impoverished childhood with an alcoholic father and absent mother. My drive and purpose in life was the next college degree for advancement in the work world. "Home" for me as a child was a place to be endured, unpredictable, at times dangerous, and pervasively empty. As the oldest child, and a bright one at that, I yearned for the sensibility of family and the comfort of nurture. I recall so clearly that more than anything else, I craved the understanding of the spiritual. From an early age, I knew there was Someone to whom I owed allegiance, whose way was right in this world.

School was my salvation—the steady, dependable, safe place. Teachers cared, and I had friends, some from the earliest of elementary school days. It was one of those girlfriends whose family were regular members in attendance at the local Baptist church. She was active at this church in a large and lively high-school-aged youth group. The church held a week-long series of revival meetings, and she thought to invite me. I walked the mile and a half to the church and back along a cold and snowy rural highway for three evenings.

On the fourth, during the altar call, I walked forward to receive and affirm Christ as my Lord and Savior, and then I walked back home.

I lived on Bible tracts, the literature given to new converts, and *Our Daily Bread*. The only visible elements of religious materials in our home were a plastic crucifix, a Catholic Missal, and a collection of Jehovah's Witness pamphlets and magazines, a remnant from the weekly meetings when my mother studied with an itinerant Jehovah's Witness missionary. From time to time, being careful not to arouse my parents' suspicions and under the guise of a "special event," I attended my friend's church. Away at college, I came under the care of a vibrant local Baptist church with a campus ministry that nurtured and tended my fledgling faith, enfolding me in its congregational life. Looking back now on this period, I am overcome with gratitude and thankfulness that the Lord preserved and sustained me in his mercy and for his purposes.

Then forty years later to be swept into a warm, lively, and vivid family life through the work and ministry of a motherly pious woman! I was embraced and shown the love of Christ, adopted, and confirmed in the love of the brethren and in the love of Grandma. Leona's remarkable ministry in letters reveals a storehouse of Christlike living accumulated throughout her life. Her letters reveal the depth and breadth of her heart and soul that compelled her loving acts of faithful service. She carried on her letter-writing ministry for more than thirty years. Her two-page letters were handwritten on a letter-size legal pad and copied double-sided. Envelopes were hand-addressed and stamped with postal commemorative stamps Grandma thought her readers would enjoy. For a woman who did not graduate high school, she shows a wonderfully skilled use of language and expression. Throughout her life, she was an author: essays and articles submitted for publication in magazines and periodicals, scripts for Sunday school plays and performances. She always gave praise and glory to God and brought comfort and encouragement to many through Scripture quotes, hymns, and words of grace.

Her practice and discipline of writing developed out of her life circumstances. Leona and Ronald's first home was in Council Bluffs, Iowa, and they lived in a house right behind the church they attended. It was easy to take part in church activities and practical as well—Leona didn't drive a car. But the comfort and convenience of life in Council Bluffs was disrupted. Ronald decided to move the family northwest to a remote, rural settlement on the banks of the Missouri River, on Goosehaven Lane in Honey Creek, Iowa. Leona did not want to move, much less to an area without transportation. But they moved, and that was that.

Leona resumed housekeeping in a mobile home in a trailer park. She loved nature and the outdoors, and the trailer had one particularly desirable space—a detached screenhouse. She developed a steady routine which included rising early to spend time there in Bible study and prayer. This time also became her dedicated interlude for writing. It is easy to imagine Leona greeting the day, talking with the Lord, reading his Word in the communal surroundings of the awakening of nature. It is likely that her letters actually began from these daily devotions, samples of which remain from the early 1960s. In fine, even handwriting, on 6 x 9 ruled eye-ease green *Rite-Nice* steno books (25 cents each), she poured out her prayers, thoughts, observations, and praises to the Lord. I found in her archives assorted notebooks, writing tablets, and finally letter-size ruled yellow pads filled with her reflections. It is easy to speculate that letters she sent to friends and family through the years began to mirror these devotional writings. From that place was born weekly reflections on life woven with the precepts and foundations of the Christian faith.

She sent her letters to over forty recipients and always at the beginning included an original salutation. I believe that as she wrote each person's name, she thought of us lovingly and perhaps even prayed for us.

Dear Joyce:

Can you believe Christmas is just around the corner? We decorated the house early, for Amy's family came after Thanksgiving. What a joy it was to have the house filled with the voices of three little boys. Amy & Brian's strong faith has brought her through the cancer surgery and treatments. It has been a challenging year for them.

Matt. 1:23 says it all quote, Behold a virgin shall be with child and shall bring forth a son and they shall call his name Immanuel which being interpreted is God with us.

If it were not so, how else would our faith have held through this year? We humbly prepare our Christmas with joy and thanksgiving. Praising God! Giving God the Glory and as the old hymn says, Count your blessings name them one by one and you'll be surprised to see what God has done!!

On the home front Bill's fall at Amy's and the fractured ribs. His bout with pneumonia and Heidi being home with her expertise as a nurse brought him through. Praise God the doctor listened to her judgement call on medication. So as our one little great grandson says God is good! All the time!

We were not able to go to church Sunday. A mini version of a blizzard hit us that morning. Gale size winds whipped the snow and so we elected not to attempt traveling. But the brunt of the snow passed us by.

Sandy and I went to Omaha last week. We stayed overnight with a long time friend and enjoyed the fellowship of several other women. We went out for lunch then came to a friends for coffee and dessert. We made a Christmas ornament and exchanged gifts. It was a lovely afternoon. We spent the night. I think the older we get the more we treasure these times.

Tamara helped Amy drive home. Heidi drove down and met them the first night out.

Even as children, she was like a mother hen with her sisters. And she brought Rebekah. So it was indeed a joyful journey.

Amy wanted to do something special for all her neighbor women who helped her through her surgery and treatments. So Sandy and I made fourteen aprons for her to give them. We used one pattern. But different fabrics.

In Nememiah 8:10 we find the words of Ezra quote, Go your way, eat the fat, and drink the sweet, and send portions unto them for whom nothing is prepared: for this day is holy unto our Lord; neither be ye sorry; for the joy of the Lord is your strength.

So we come to our Christmas celebration. Remembering the difficulties. Praising God for His ever present help through this year. And above all thanking God for sending Jesus to draw us in.

Love you much,
Grandma Moats

These letters were penned every week, every year, for over thirty years. They were a special form of writing for her, far beyond the usual family kinds of communications of birthday cards, anniversary cards, graduation congratulations notes. In them, her hands are lifted in praise to God with thanks for his mercy and care for her family. Her heart, grateful for even the most everyday kinds of events, flowed onto the page. Portions of hymns brought grace to her mind and the minds of her readers. Scripture quotes reminded her and her readers of the loving and dependable care of our heavenly Father. These letters were to her a "double portion" of blessing: by placing on the page a retelling of God's gracious and merciful acts to her family and friends, she savored again the special favor of her Savior. From this, she expressed and lived to others the "loyal love" of God.

The letters were a ministry in the latter portion of Grandma's life. As I came to know the family and heard the bountiful history of Leona's life story, I now appreciate the scope of her Christian life. It is more—far more—than just a life of many good deeds and kindnesses to strangers. By journeying through her life and its context, we have access to a rich resource to nourish our own journey of faith. She honored and accepted the responsibility to live in a way that reflected her faith and to guide family and others on that path. She showed us the effort, study, and labor it takes to develop the disciplines of prayer and to grasp an understanding of the Scriptures—the work that is required to develop discernment in applying God's Word to life, the discovery of God's will through the contemplation of his Word. Above all, she showed us love—a living love of neighbor, loving care of family borne out of gratitude and leaving a heritage of faith as a legacy. Leona's faith manifests an awareness of the world and the Christian's relationship to it. Because of her acts of mercy and ministry to others, Christ's love is declared in his creation in this sphere.

This loving response to God's grace—unmerited favor—is recorded in historical accounts in the Word of God. One such account is set down in the book of Ruth. Among the saints of old, there could be no two less desperate and indigent people than Ruth and her mother-in-law Naomi. They were providentially brought into the realm of Boaz's life, a prosperous and well-regarded farmer. Naomi discerned that Boaz might serve as a "kinsman redeemer" for her family—one who "comes alongside," one who shows respect and kindness, who fulfills the responsibility to promote the well-being of another, one who acts on behalf of someone in need. Boaz was simply living out his Hebrew faith, behaving in accordance with the concept of *hesed*, a practice of merciful, compassionate, grace-filled lovingkindness to others.

Compassionate attitudes toward others alludes to the character of God in his work of redemption, a poignant picture of salvation. *Hesed* is a central precept of theology, saturating the Scriptures from beginning to end. It is a key attribute of the Lord's character, active in our redemption and salvation, and becomes an identifying mark of

God's covenant community. Utterly faithful to his people, the highest expression of the Lord's *hesed* is Jesus, whose suffering on the cross and victory over sin and death makes visible the ultimate merciful love and redemption.

A word majestic in its complexity and richness, *hesed* carries with it the dual components of the Lord's faithful love and loyalty and, thenceforth, the expectation that his people shall love their neighbor in thoughts, actions, deeds, and in service to them. As Grandma would point out, Micah 6:8 declares,

> He has shown you, O man, what is good;
> And what does the Lord require of you
> But to do justly,
> To love mercy,
> And to walk humbly with your God? (NKJV)

"Love" and "loyalty" combined in acts of service, mercy, and kindness—our calling in this life is to practice this loyal love, loving our neighbor as ourselves and as the Lord loves us. While we extend mercy and gracious service to all who ask it of us, there is a special connection to those adopted into the family of God through Christ and united by the bond of faith. The covenant community—our true family—is not just bloodline connections, but that commonwealth created when we are united to God through Jesus Christ.

The story of Ruth and Boaz is one of many narratives throughout Scripture that the Lord uses to portray his precepts by which we, his people, should desire and ought to live. What if *we* lived *today* in "loyal love" to the Lord with true *hesed*, "redeeming one another?" What would that look like? I am convinced with much certainty that it would look like Grandma's life. And I have more than a thousand letters as evidence and inspiration to prove it.

CHAPTER 2

In Her Own Words

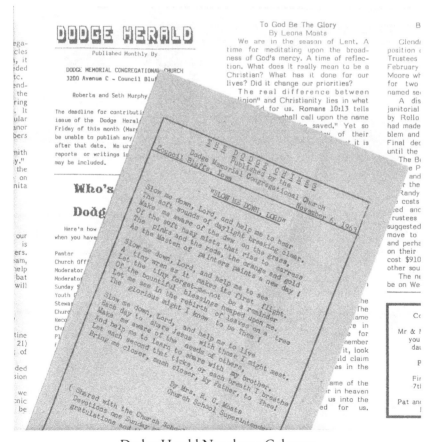

Dodge Herald Newsletter Columns

We are given gifts. We are called to serve the Lord and his church with the gifts he has given us for the good and well-being of all. First Corinthians 12 makes clear the church's teaching that we serve one another in our covenant communities, in our jobs, in the cities and towns where we live, and in the world—as we are given the opportunity. For those given the gift of service, as Leona was, the Lord Jesus's command in Matthew 22:27–30 to love one's neighbor meant to employ one's time and talent in ministering the love of the Lord Jesus to others, and included in that service was her talent as a writer.

The archived materials of Leona's life fit into a standard-sized eighteen by twenty-four inches plastic storage bin. Among the artifacts is evidence of a robust and wide-ranging production of writing for many different purposes and audiences. In my hands are typewritten copies of stories and essays dating back to 1963. There are memoir pieces and short fiction. She wrote essays on Christian living and opinion pieces on Christianity and its relationship to current cultural events. Her submissions traveled to *Guideposts*, *The War Cry* (official publication of the Salvation Army), and likely to *The International Journal of Religious Education*. There is a rejection letter from the *Christian Herald Magazine* in New York. She wrote inspirational passages for *The Dodge Chimes*, and later *The Dodge Herald*, monthly newsletters for the Dodge Memorial Congregational Church in Council Bluffs, her home church. Serving as Sunday school superintendent for this church for many years, she wrote scripts for children's Easter and Christmas programs. And this lowly plastic box, this repository of a life's work, is filled with hundreds of daily devotional writings that became a ministry of hope and comfort to a select audience of family and friends.

I am led to ponder how such an inclination toward writing was cultivated and encouraged in Leona's life. Did this affection arise from time spent as an avid reader? Was it nurtured in her home life, in school, or as a part of family history? At the bottom of the plastic storage bin are two slim journals. They are "remembrance books" designed for a family member to write and record for posterity information on his or her life. Lovely hardcover volumes, these books are a cross between a scrapbook—with artwork, graphics, and sections for photographs or other mementoes—and an appealing and colorful children's picture book. Perhaps they were given to Leona as gifts from a grandchild, for each asks for written responses to questions about a *grandmother's* life. The woman who wrote thousands of pages of letters about the life of her family, loved ones, and beloved Savior was asked—twice—to record the significant details surrounding her own life. How fortunate we are that she did, for this unassuming woman, who thought her life ordinary and unremarkable, traces her family life back to covered-wagon days and settlement of the West in the United States. She recounts wistfully the school days and her best school subjects, interests used by the Lord which culminated in her lifelong affection for and ministry in writing. She remembers the cryptic details of her own salvation experience. In her own words is the remarkable life story of Leona's place in this world.

Each remembrance book begins with Leona's place of birth and date. Leona Mae Smith was born January 6, 1921, in Missouri Valley, Iowa, to Clifford and Mabel Smith.

> I was born in my grandparent's home with a doctor and midwife in attendance. We had water in the house but an outhouse for a bathroom toilet. A spotted dog ran between my mother's legs on her trip outside (and brought on labor.) When she first saw me, I had brown stuff around my eyes and a pointed head from the long labor. She cried because she thought she had marked me. The midwife gently shaped my head and assured her I was fine.

Clifford Carroll Smith and Mabel Alvira Butcher Smith

Mabel Alvira Butcher, Leona's mother, was born in Missouri Valley, Iowa, on April 18, 1901. She was one of nine children and during her childhood was sent to Council Bluffs to live with a couple affectionately known (though unrelated) as Grandma and Grandpa Cookie. Mabel went to work for a Kresge's dime store in Council Bluffs, where she became friends with a young woman named Leona Smith. Leona introduced Mabel to her brother Clifford Carroll Smith. Mabel and Clifford were married in September 1919, and together they moved to Missouri Valley, where Clifford plied his trade as a hide and fur buyer. Leona Mae Smith was named for Clifford's sister Leona, and in 1923, Ella Marie, Leona Mae's sister, was born, named for Mabel's sister. It was a time in our country when families cherished their lineage and preserved the connections through the generations with beloved family names.

George McClelland Butcher and Nettie Webster Butcher

Leona Mae and Ella Marie knew their grandparents, whose histories mirrored the rough-and-tumble character of the United States during the latter part of the nineteenth century. Mabel's mother, Nettie Webster Butcher, was one of ten children, her nine siblings all brothers. A devout Baptist, she was well known throughout the town for her ministry to local families with sickness or need. George McClelland Butcher, Mabel's father, was the town marshal in Missouri Valley, where they lived. George Butcher was, in the words of one newspaper writer, a "good, whole-souled man." He was called by the Chicago & North Western Railway Company to investigate the hobo camp down in the rail yards as there were suspected burglars and fugitives in the camp. George Butcher was shot and killed in August 1912 while attempting to apprehend one of the hoboes, an event which launched a posse of over 150 men in search of the killer and his accomplice. The local paper followed the progress of the manhunt closely, and it became a storied chapter in Missouri Valley's history. The fugitives were found three days later, mysteriously bound and drowned in the Missouri River, near Honey Creek, Iowa. George Butcher left behind his wife, Nettie, and six living children. She raised that family on her own without the help of a pension or other social supports, sending the youngest two children to college.

Clifford's father, George Smith, a Scots-Irish immigrant, found his way to Council Bluffs in the late nineteenth century, making at least a portion of the trip in a covered prairie wagon. He met the petite Ella Smith (whose mother was Chinook Indian) from Erie Pennsylvania, and they made their home in Council Bluffs. During this time of rapid exploration, homesteading, and expansion of the West, true pioneers such as George and Ella made their home and living within the opportunities in front of them. George farmed but was mainly a contractor, building roads in the vicinity of Council Bluffs. In the late 1800s, the Council Bluffs area experienced an explosion of growth in the railroad industry, with companies springing up overnight and miles of track being laid. With an entrepreneurial spirit, George and Ella followed the crews laying track, making and selling breakfasts to them.

By the 1920s and the years of Leona Mae's and Ella Marie's childhoods, the Council Bluffs area grew and prospered as a railroad hub of the Great Plains. Still families lived in modest circumstances, and the children learned to be satisfied with simple provisions and entertainments.

> I had an (older) half sister named Lily and a sister named Ella Marie. We girls shared a room and I slept with my younger sister. The only heat in the room was a floor register over the living room. When we took a bath Saturday night Mother had a little kerosene heater to warm the bathroom with. My mother entered a chocolate cake in the county fair, and won a hot water heater from the gas company. They even installed it for us. We had two changes of longjohns in the winter. One we wore all week and the other in the wash.

I never had my own bed let alone a blanket. But my Grandma Butcher gave me a new cedar chest when I was two. As a teenager she put things in it for me. A lovely cutglass set of goblets and a pitcher, sugar bowl, and creamer. I still have them.

Mother used to put me outside on a quilt with my older (step)sister. We had little celluloid dolls. We spent hours in the shade in the summertime making clothes for our dolls. We kept them in a cigar box.

I received a Bylo Baby Doll when I was almost five. It had a china head and I dearly loved it. It was complete with a frog leg body. My sister broke hers…one day she grabbed my doll and swung it around. It hit the bannister and broke. I cried and cried. My next doll was a big baby doll and a wicker buggy. I had it until Sandy found it in the closet. She played with it for years. And we used to cut paper dolls out of catalogs, furniture and all.

Thus began Leona's lifelong love for dolls, and she added to her collection of antique bisque and celluloid dolls throughout her life.

Leona and her sisters spent time outdoors in activities by themselves and with neighborhood children. Sometimes the activities were solitary and imaginative and at other times part of the communal childhood neighborhood bustle.

I used to love to lie in the shade and watch the clouds. I could always see lovely forms and shapes in the clouds and wove stories around them to entertain my younger cousins. We made kites out of newspapers and twine. The tails were scraps of material tied in knots.

One year my sister and I wanted bikes. Mother told me they couldn't afford two and said because she was younger would I mind if she got one? She said I could ride it when Ella wasn't. That was always at night. It didn't have lights but I rode it anyway.

We lived on the streetcar line. We'd play base-ball in the street. But we always quit when a street-car came by. I couldn't hit the broad side of a barn. But one day the pitcher tossed a ball and to my hor-ror I connected with it. It went right through a top window (of the streetcar.) I ran in to Mother crying and a neighbor girl followed me to say I'd surely go to jail. I was so frightened. But nothing happened.

Wintertime activities were outdoors, local, simple, and homemade.

We had a sled. Dad would shovel the snow in a pile so we could slide down it. A friend's uncle flooded a vacant lot by building a dirt dike and the city would flood it. I never learned to ice skate but I loved to slide on it and fell into the airhole once. My friend's mother dried my clothes by her coal heater and ironed them. She then took me home late and explained to my mother. We didn't have a phone.

Most families have holiday traditions, and despite the mod-est circumstances of her family Leona remembered fondly Easter, Thanksgiving, and Christmas celebrations.

Mother was a very good cook and loved to fix big meals for holidays. She was good at feed-ing us on a very slim budget. The only spaghetti I knew was made with onion, bacon, and a can of tomatoes. We sometimes had milk and corn-bread for supper.

Mother always made my sister and I a new dress (for Easter.) I don't remember having an egg hunt, but we always got to take our long under-wear off on Easter whether Easter was early or late.

Years later, in my own family, church was the center of our lives and the children grew up knowing Jesus first. Others second. Ourselves last. So Easter from Sunrise Service to family din-ner was a joyful time.

(Thanksgiving in my childhood) was a fam-ily time and Mother's family came to our house. Then the Financial Crash (Great Depression) changed that. No one could afford to travel. When the family couldn't come Mother started inviting people who were alone. We'd always have two or three extras and we never knew who it would be. Somehow turkey would be the main dish with dressing and mash potatoes, vegetables and pie.

At Christmas we had a stocking and it was the one time we got a big apple and an orange. My Mother would buy my Father an inexpensive mechanical toy because he never had a toy (as a child.) One time she and my aunt got a little donkey pulling a cart. The driver had a bucket hanging over his head. They wound it up and it would go forward, backward, in circles. They wore the first one out and had to get Dad another one. Gifts for my family were ones that I made at school.

Gifts—those we give and those we are given. Whatever may be our inclinations, interests, and talents that we share with others, they seem first to spring from gifts given to us. As it turns out, the schools Leona attended as a child and young woman were among the best in the newly settled West, despite the Council Bluffs area's early reputation as a wild, rugged, and unruly frontier town.

Council Bluffs was named by Lewis and Clark, who were on their way westward along the Missouri River to explore and establish a presence in the newly acquired Louisiana Purchase. The site commemorates a meeting in August 1804 with the Otoe Native American tribe. In the 1830s, an area of land south and east of this meeting place, on the east side of the Missouri River, became reservation lands for Potawatomi, Chippewa, and Ottawa tribes in the region. In the 1830s through the 1840s, many Native Americans were pushed from the Chicago area to this region; by the late 1840s, they were pushed even further west to new reservations established in Kansas, opening the Council Bluffs region for pioneer settlement.

Council Bluffs held an enormous advantage: a steam-powered ferry existed to shuttle goods and livestock across the river. This was a major factor in making Council Bluffs the starting point for immigrant trails, the most notable of which is the Mormon Trail (and later the easternmost terminus of the Transcontinental Railroad.) In the mid-1840s, Council Bluffs, renamed Kanesville at that time, experienced a large influx of Mormons, who were moving through the area westward to Utah along what became known as the Mormon Trail. During the rapid convergence of pioneers in preparation for that migration, in 1847, the Mormon population divided Kanesville into four "wards" and established a private school in each ward. Soon afterward, the majority of the Mormon population departed the region; and in 1853, Kanesville became Council Bluffs once again. In 1859, voters created the Council Bluffs public school system, building schools and providing education in a deliberate manner. In 1866, the first school was built, named the First Ward School. This school was later renamed Bloomer School and was the first school Leona attended. She attended Franklin and Longfellow elementary schools, and Abraham Lincoln High School, built in 1871, was Leona's first high school. She spent her last year in school at Thomas Jefferson

High School, built in 1921. By 1930, the middle of Leona's school career, enrollment in the Council Bluffs public schools topped ten thousand students. Each of the schools Leona attended—Bloomer, Franklin, Longfellow, Abraham Lincoln High School, and Thomas Jefferson High School—are still in existence and serving students today.

Leona remembered special teachers and her favorite school subjects. Once she finished school, she thought she might like to become an airline stewardess.

> There were many special teachers, but one in particular made an impression. Her name was Miss Pike. I always admired her shoes. She always had them shined. I would take my 10 cents for lunch in 9th grade and get my shoes shined.
>
> My favorite subjects were Ancient History and Literary English. The Lord uses that now to write letters to people who need to know he loves them.

Despite her love for literature and school, Leona Mae Smith, however, did not graduate from high school. A life-changing event intervened.

> I met your grandfather, Ronald Charles Moats, at a dance. He was born in Missouri Valley, Iowa on January 12, 1917. I was sixteen, and he was twenty. I thought he was the cutest thing but I didn't like him. He liked to tease me. He knew I was extremely shy. But he could make me laugh. My mom liked him.
>
> Our first date we went with another couple to a rodeo in Shenandoah. It was Depression times so we went to shows. A night out was to be able to stop for a 20 cent pork tenderloin (sandwich) after the show. We went to wienie roasts,

picnics, and rodeos. Took in carnivals and went fishing. We dated a year. He kept asking me and I told him one day you will ask too often. And he did. I never regretted it.

We eloped. We were married on July 24, 1939. I wore a summer dress; it was very hot that day. We went first to Papillion (Sarpy County Courthouse, in Nebraska) and found I was too young at eighteen. Drove over to Glenwood (courthouse, Glenwood, Iowa.) The judge was holding court; one of our friends picked the flowers on the court house yard. So we came back to Council Bluffs and got married there. Our friends Bob and Juanita Clark celebrated our wedding day with us.

We lived in Council Bluffs. Ronald's father made an apartment upstairs in his house for us and we lived there three years before buying a house at 2308 Avenue G. My parents both died within a few years and I loved my in-laws very much. Ronald drove a cab until he finally went to work for the Union Pacific Railroad. I worked for a family. They had one little boy. I loved to keep house, as my mother sternly taught me when I was a child. When I quit they had another boy and I had my daughter.

Sandra Joyce (whom we called Sandy Jo) was born on November 24, 1940. An adorable little girl whose aunt and uncles really spoiled. Church was the first place I took her. She grew up loving Jesus. Her penchant in life was doing nice things for other people. Often they weren't aware of who did it. Like the time she made a new skirt for a girl who wasn't even nice to her because the 8th graders were graduating and Martha didn't have anything new to wear. She never knew where it came from. That's been the story of her life.

Remembrance books provide a format of questions designed to give a picture of a family's structure and life. The format does not address all the particular nuances for a family especially subjects like Leona's deep Christian faith. Between the two slim books, I found only one quintessential, noteworthy, pithy line, elegant in its simplicity:

> What memories do you have Grandma, of going to church as a child? An aunt took me to a nursery while she was in a church. I remember they had a sand box. When I was ten years old a neighbor girl took me to the Nazarene church where I gave my heart to Jesus.

That is all which is recorded in the remembrance books of Leona's conversion. But this seed bed of faith is watered, weeded, nurtured, and grown for the next eighty years. Leona's letters document an astonishing and fruitful path of faithful living in service to the One who owns her heart, Jesus Christ. The Lord's gift of her life to us becomes a benediction in our own hearts.

CHAPTER 3

The Potter and the Clay

Jan 2 2002

We stand on the threshold of a New Year. The past few months have made many rethink where their priorities are. Or realize how fragile life is, and how quickly it slips away from us. The thought brings to mind the words of the hymn Take time to be Holy. Speak oft with thy Lord. Abide in Him always. And feed on His Word. Make friends of God's children. Help those who are weak. Forgetting in nothing His Blessing to seek.

Feed on his Word. How often when we are reading the Bible does a scripture meet a need in our life. Or gives us something to share with someone else. In the study of Col. 3:16 stood out. Quote. And let the peace of God dwell in you richly in all wisdom, teaching and admonishing one another in psalms and hymns and spiritual songs, singing with grace in your hearts to the Lord.

The words, let the peace of God dwell in you. How often over the years have we experienced that peace inspite of the things going on in our lives or the life of someone dear to us? We literally sense the presence of God and find the strength, the patience, the wisdom that could only come from the Lord himself.

Mine is a simple kind of faith that has never questioned the power of the Holy Spirit spoken of in Luke 1: 35-36. It was a joy to read Luke 1.37 For with God nothing shall be impossible.

That the Lord doesn't work on our time table isn't important. My granddaughters answer to this is Lord what are you trying to teach me now?

Life can be a challenge. It can even threaten to overwhelm

A Handwritten Letter

The Great Depression of the 1930s touched the life of every American. Leona was in her early teens when the privations and restrictions of that time made their way into her family's life. Despite the leanness of those years, Leona recalled with fondness the "make do" spirit of her parents' and grandparents' determined efforts to provide a loving home.

> My father taught me to love my grandparents. My mother taught me to value integrity and to be honest, and even in the hardness of the Depression, she managed to provide special blessings for Christmas and my birthday.

As all young girls during that "coming of age" time in her life, Leona kept up with the world of entertainment and music. In the aftermath of World War I and the enveloping doom of the Depression, entertainment provided relief from the suffocating dreariness of daily life. By the early 1930s, "talkies" were the standard for motion pictures, and color films made inroads as the decade wore on. Leona's favorite actor was Clark Gable, and her favorite actress was Carol Lombard. A reader, Leona's favorite books were *The Story of Penelope Stout* (1897) by Thomas Hale Streets and *Heidi* (1881) by Johanna Spyri. In the evenings, she and her family listened to the *Amos & Andy* nightly radio serial drama broadcast on NBC Radio. To take a vacation was an unimaginable luxury, but Leona found refuge and welcoming arms at her Grandmother Butcher's home in Council Bluffs and often spent time there. By far, Leona's greatest delights were the celebration of the holidays especially Christmas "when all the family came." From childhood, when gifts to her were an apple and an orange in her Christmas stocking, to becoming the family matriarch and center of Christmas celebration, Grandma loved every element of the season of Christ's birth. Her family inevitably grew, and branches took root in many parts of the country. She longed for and expected family to gather under her roof and at her table so she might preside over the festivities. A heightened sense of poignancy and joy pervades her letters at Christmastime.

Dear Joyce:

We have been busy making candy and cookies for the company we expect to come. I'm not sure the granddaughters, who are health conscious, and weight, will thank us for the temptation. Curious it occurred to me life has many choices. One important thing that stays in my subconscious mind is the fact that we can never save a soul. Only God can do that. Still by prayer and example others may come to the saving grace and knowledge of Christ. Submission to our circumstances may be an opportunity to let our light shine for Jesus. Jesus said in Matthew 5:14, Ye are the light of the world…and in v. 16: Let your light so shine before men, that they may see your good works and glorify your Father in Heaven. So time, age, and health may open a door to share Jesus. One of the most beautiful truths of the Bible is found in Jeremiah 18:4. And the vessel that he made of clay was marred in the hand of the potter, so he made it again another vessel as it seemed good to the potter to make. It is comforting at this time in my life my God is able to shape me and mold me into a vessel he can use to comfort or encourage others.

I wonder if Mary had those thoughts after the visitation of the Angel. It was beyond her understanding. But her willingness to be God's vessel is a wonderful example for us today. Can we accept the limitations age and health put on us? Or do we waste time in pity? God forbid. We may miss a wonderful opportunity to let our light be a pathway for another. The thought of those shepherds tending their flocks on that awesome night when Christ was born. Luke 2:10, 11: And the angel said unto them Fear not, for behold I bring you good tidings of great joy which shall be to all people. For unto you is born this day in the city of David, a savior which is Christ the Lord. And this shall be a sign unto you. You shall find the babe in swaddling clothes lying in a manger. Oh joy of joy that is our hope beyond the present days. But for now we are challenged to let our light shine for the purpose of glorifying our Father in Heaven.

Wow! How exciting can life be! My family had a Christmas Open House this week and we were blessed to have new neighbors and friends from church come. It was a wonderful time to get to make new friends.

I've been on the cookie baking detail and Sandy on the candy. We keep the kitchen busy and the house full of sweet scents. When I wear thin Sandy takes over. And Bill has even made our meals for us. God is so good!!

So life brings change. But God can still make something beautiful out of a worn-out piece of clay if we submit our will to his will.

Love you much, Grandma Moats

On another occasion, she writes,

Christmas has become a memory in the book of life. One of the most pleasant memories is the candlelight service Sunday evening. Only candles were used to light the sanctuary. It added a sense of reverence and beauty in the stillness that filled the room. The stillness in the sanctuary filled me with a peace, yet a feeling of expectancy and I felt the presence of the Lord. Maybe that is what Anna the prophetess felt when she came into the sanctuary that day Luke 3:38 and she began to give thanks unto the Lord. I never thought much about how old I am until I suddenly realized I had crossed the seventy plus ten. The expectations of the future with Jesus is uppermost in my mind. But urgency to make a difference in someone's life or future is uppermost in my heart… As we walked around lighting one another's candles I prayed, Lord, let each day count for you and keep me sensitive to the needs of others. Help me not to miss an opportunity to comfort or encourage someone today. We really don't know how many tomorrows we have. So today is important, and we leave our tomorrows in God's hands.

We had twenty-nine for dinner. One coming from Florida with his wife. And the grandson's family from South Dakota. As we came before God to praise him and ask his blessing on our food and fellowship, it was a joy to be able to thank him for his Presence in their lives and for allowing this time together.

As Leona faces life after the "seventy plus ten," possessions become fewer. Her home is sold, and she makes the inevitable move to apartment living. She indulges a lifelong desire for travel. The travel now has a more urgent purpose: spending the rich, loving time with a growing extended family and receiving the necessary care and companionship in return. Not one to waste opportunity to "let our light be a pathway for another," she applies the light of a lifetime of acquired wisdom, serving others and looking to Jesus, the Author and Finisher of our faith. Her writing reveals sensitivity to the more profound meanings taught in Scripture.

Grandma's age and wisdom granted her an awareness of the undeniable advance of the pace of life and the irresistible march of change. This realization comes with the assurance, through the influence of the Holy Spirit and the discernment of living, that God can make something out of clay that seems marred by the potter. As Grandma says with conviction and by example,

> It is comforting at this time in my life my God is able to shape me and mold me into a vessel he can use to comfort and encourage others.

A long-lived life in service to others reveals a beauty of the soul and the fruitfulness of faith. It is a means of change not just in others but also in ourselves. Emptiness is evident in the self-gratification and selfish ambitions permeating our culture. The words penned by Leona Moats turn us back and slow us down to a focus of glorifying God and serving others. She marveled at that. Then she got to work living it, and she left behind a record of it.

We are challenged to "let our light shine" to glorify our heavenly Father. We do so by being of service to others. This way of family life, led by a devout matriarch, captures my heart. It is a beautiful foreign land in contrast to my own youth and family life. I yearn for it to become a part of my spirit and soul.

My mother was born in 1921, the same year as Leona's birth. The coal-mining towns and miner families of western Pennsylvania faced the same hardships as those hardworking families in the breadbasket of America in Iowa. An orange or an apple or a pair of socks were perhaps the most a child of those times and in those places could expect for a Christmas gift.

My mother's childhood was spent in a coal mining camp southwest of Pittsburgh during the years of the Great Depression. As the Depression deepened, the mining industry suffered decline as demand for coal and coke products waned. The great blast furnaces of Pittsburgh and Cleveland produced less steel and other products in the depths of the economic slowdown. Mine companies that managed to remain open reduced work weeks to two days per week or even to one. In those years, the miner's family Christmas tree, if there even was one, sometimes had no gifts under it.

I am trying to understand this legacy I have been bequeathed, a time now nearly one hundred years ago. My mother's insistence upon taking her daughters back to the "old home place" was never explained. It was simply expected that we would absorb through the storytelling and the very air we breathed in those Pennsylvania hollas, the profound courage and strength needed to survive and meet the challenges in this world. It was the best she could do to prepare us for the future. Perhaps all parents know that in one way or another, they must hand down the wisdom and experience of the past to their children and their children's children to fulfill instinctive responsibilities to coming generations. I became curious and reflective, and it led me to think more deeply about the steep, wooded Pennsylvania hillsides, the stone quarries and the mine shafts, the blast furnaces, and the raw industrial thirst of the mining and railroad companies along the spine of the Appalachian Mountains in the eastern United States.

In a thought-provoking work by Joanna K. Stratton[1], *Pioneer Women: Voices from the Kansas Frontier*, the esteemed historian Arthur M. Schlesinger, Jr. is quoted as saying, "History is lived in the main by the unknown and forgotten." Stratton's heroines in her story, the "unknown and forgotten," are the women who shouldered fully half the burden of carving a life for their families in the settlement of the vast and unbroken prairies of the West in the 1800s. How similar were the experiences of the women who, as immigrants from England, Scotland, Czechoslovakia, Yugoslavia, Poland, Lithuania, and Italy followed their men as they searched for work and a new life in America in the vast coal patches that stretched from northern Pennsylvania southward through eastern Ohio, western West Virginia, Virginia, and eastern Kentucky. The coal patches spawned

---

[1] Joanna L. Stratton writes a compelling, detailed historical portrait surrounding the lives of women on the American frontier in Kansas. She draws from over 800 handwritten, first-person letters collected by her great-grandmother Lilla Day Monroe. Her book completes her great-grandmother's cherished project to leave a legacy of the pioneer woman's experiences, perseverance, devotion, and ingenuity.

"coal camps," company towns created and supported by the mining companies in the rural and remote areas in which the mines were established. It is an iconic era in American life, documented and interpreted in tenacious, gritty museums throughout the coal region, in personal memoirs and in books dedicated to the remembrance and preservation of this obscure culture. The scars of mining operations in the coal patches remain, as do many of the coal camps that survive today as towns.

In the Allegheny Mountains of western Pennsylvania, towns by the name of Ernest, Clymer, Lucerne, Iselin, Sagamore, Cuddy, Arcadia, and Wilgus and so many others took root. The Connellsville coal and coke region, a rich deposit of high-quality coal and a product called beehive coke, angles from north to south through western Pennsylvania. In an era spanning roughly the 1870s through the late 1970s, mining companies small and large scrambled to stake claims on land under which lay the "black gold" of coal, promising great wealth. Much of this coal was converted to a product called coke. Among the largest companies was the Rochester & Pittsburgh Coal & Iron Company, supplying the coal and coke to fuel the blast furnaces of the steel industry in Pittsburgh.

Once a mine site was identified, the mining company moved quickly to establish operations. Rail lines and transportation infrastructure were erected quickly. Workers were recruited from other existing company mines, often in England, Scotland, and eastern Europe, and thus the "immigrant" culture of the operations was commonplace. Because the coal patches occupied undeveloped rural areas, "coal camps" were built, sometimes with amazing speed, to provide for the living necessities of the workforce. The company towns varied in the care and attention to amenities, but many included the construction of schools, a community hall, and churches.

Houses built for the miners' families were simple frame construction. Typically, these houses had no running water, no electricity, coal (or wood) for stoves for heating and cooking, and outhouses. This was the 1900s in our country. The coal camps varied widely, depending upon the particular mining company and its interest in the welfare of its miners and their families. Some companies provided little more than the house itself. Others assigned company engineers to plan out the community. Families were provided communal water pumps near the miner's houses (water was pumped by hand and carried inside for use), coal for fuel, and electricity from the mine power station though few families could afford labor-saving electric appliances. Very few homes had indoor bathrooms. Thus, an archetypal bathing ritual was established: when the miner came home in the evenings covered with coal dirt, a zinc tub was placed on the floor in the kitchen. Hot water from the coal stove's water reservoir filled the tub and was replenished periodically as the miner completed his bath. So laborious was the bathing ritual that most miners' family's descendants recall that as children they were afforded only the once-a-week "Saturday night bath."

Miners and their families were European immigrants, who brought with them traditions and practices of "the old country." It was common for women to expect to have a neighborhood outdoor brick oven where they could carry on the communal tradition of baking bread. These ovens were built by Italian immigrant coal miners, who used the same expert stonemason skills acquired in the old country to build the cavernous round beehive coke ovens for the mine operations.

In the southwestern Pennsylvania camps of my mother's youth, ethnicity was expressed in the traditional cultural foods and preservation techniques especially meats. Nearly every family had a garden. In some camps, families were permitted to keep livestock—cows, chickens, and pigs. Canning and food preservation were essential to survival. Nothing went to waste—not even the pin feathers of the fowl. Thereupon was born the legendary "feathertick." The down and soft feathers of ducks and chickens were saved and made into thick, fluffy comforters that were very warm. Most houses were unheated upstairs, and most coal miner's children, like my mother, relate stories of sleeping snugly with siblings, three or four to a bed, under the featherticks.

Women worked hard to make homes for their families during the Depression years in the 1930s. The mining slowdown and the economic deprivation of those years taxed the creativity and fortitude of many a miner's wife. Washing clothes was a particularly arduous task due to the necessity of pumping, carrying, and heating water. Coal dust is abrasive and has a greasy quality that made this task, carried out in tubs and on washboards, time-consuming and strenuous. Despite the labor involved, some women would take in wash from the bachelor miners in the camp in order to earn a few extra cents for the family.

Miner's wives fitted and sewed homemade and handmade clothing for themselves and their children. The sturdy and ubiquitous treadle sewing machine, if the family was fortunate enough to have one, earned its keep for the making of all manner of household needs—from underwear and children's clothes to sheets, pillowcases, curtains, dishtowels, and quilts. My grandmother's circa 1900 White treadle sewing machine, in a solid-oak cabinet, survives from this era. Having been passed down first to my mother, it now rests from its labors in my sewing room. Materials consisted of flour sack or potato sack cloth or the only other fabric available from the company store—"mine muslin." This muslin was a sturdy, coarse cotton sheeting and was used in the mines to block off dangerous or unused areas and sometimes to wrap the bodies of miners injured or even killed in mine accidents. Families of this era were often large compared to today's standards—there were more than a dozen children in my mother's—so it was an accepted practice that clothing was handed down within families from child to child until completely worn out. Clothing such as black garments worn for funerals was even shared among neighbors. Schoolgirls generally had two dresses—one in the wash and one on her back, a note of startling interest to me. A crystal-clear memory of my own lean childhood is of the ritual visit in August, in preparation for the start of school, to the Buster Brown's children's clothing store on 14 Mile Road in Clawson, Michigan. My mother would select two dresses each for my sister and me. During our elementary school years, those dresses lasted the entire year. We wore one while each day she washed the other one to be worn the next day. She simply carried on the tradition and frugality of her own youth. Later, the sewing skills I learned in eighth-grade home economics class equipped me to sew on my mother's electric

Montgomery Ward sewing machine, the small wardrobe I wore to school each day, the only clothing I had.

While we did not know it then, the few brief years in which we paid family visits to the "old home place" in Pennsylvania were effective in planting the seeds of legacy. Those of my mother's generation lived through momentous and swift changes as the twentieth century unfolded through the 1940s, 1950s, and 1960s. Legacy is a gift of connection across generations. Our ancestors confirm that an understanding of the past serves as a place to find courage and strength to meet our own challenges. The lives and testimonies of others are a light unto our path which, in its best sense, propels us forward in our search for the shape, value, and meaning of our own lives.

In the last years of her life, my mother lives as a recluse, her home slowly becoming a fortress in which the light of life through friends and eventually family could not penetrate. Holidays come and go without the celebrations of meals of her ethnic Slovenian specialties. Defiantly independent, the inevitable medical emergency forces the issue of her continuing to live alone. With little discussion or resistance, she is resigned to the relentless march of growing old. I move her to nursing home care at a wonderful, attentive facility not far from her last home.

The halls this Christmas morning are festive, bright, and full of the cheer of holiday decorations. A Christmas tree claims a tiny corner in my mother's cubicle room, with paper ornaments and greetings from 3rd-floor staff. There is a Menorah and similar greetings for my mother's Jewish roommate, Sarah. My mother seldom leaves her bed in her semiprivate room. She is always bathed and dressed in clean clothing well before the arrival of breakfast. Today she wears her favorite T-shirt, a folk-art stencil of cardinals in their nest box home, and flannel pants. She receives the first of several daily visits from a lively button-eyed little bichon frise, who seems to have claimed my mother as his favorite client. The nursing home staff bring their pets to work, employing them in a well-regarded practice of the warmth and therapeutic value of companion animals. He leaps upon her bed for several minutes of petting and stroking then dashes off out the door and down the hallway to his next "appointment." Though I could take her by wheelchair down to the dining room, we remain in my mother's room. Our Christmas luncheon tray arrives, a substantial plate of turkey and dressing, with her favorite cheesecake for dessert. I cut portions and prepare her meal. We spend the time mostly in silence, watching a basketball game on the television. We do the best we can.

My mother was eighty-nine when she passed from this life in 2012. Leona was ninety-five at her passing in 2016. I consider the grace bestowed upon each of them the gift of long lives spanning significant historical periods and monumental cultural shifts.

My mother made her way on her own, adapting and surviving with the grit and determination borne in her bones, drawing only upon that legacy which was given her in the circumstances of her birthplace. She seldom recognized the merciful rule and sustaining power of the Lord of life. Alone in an absolute sense most of her life, she governed her family from that place of aloneness. Though my mother's and father's families included eleven siblings on each side, we were never a part of large tribal gatherings. I never really knew my aunts, uncles, cousins; the fellowship and love of kin never made its way into our house. My mother lived a life outside the security of abiding in a community of faith or family. She left me on my own to make my way through my own history, outside a family's care, always searching for that care.

Leona surely recognized the hands of the Potter upon her life. Blessed by the sovereign Lord who does with his creation as he wills, he shaped her clay into a vessel fit for the honor of serving him faithfully within those members of familial kinship, among those of the household of faith adopted into the family of God and the stranger in need of a smile or a kind word. Taking Jesus as her abiding companion, Leona never found herself alone.

In the Lord's providence, my life's work became that of ministering to families, the giving away of one's self in the nurture and care of others. In this work, I had always the sense of being an outsider. But in his perfect timing, I was swept into the embrace of the loving forever family, the family of God, and then welcomed into the breadth and reach of Leona's open arms through her writing. This experience is a joyful down payment, here in the present, of the glorious familial Light and Presence in which we shall dwell in the ages to come.

CHAPTER 4

Writing Is a Calling

Leona Mae Smith

Writing is a calling. If I had the privilege of asking Grandma why she wrote with such discipline, devotion, and intention, she might have directed me down many different paths. Perhaps she admired the stories she read in childhood and in school, and the muse captured her imagination. Perhaps she grew to appreciate the cadence, rhythm, and beauty of words on the page. She may have esteemed an author's skill in creation of pictures and scenes in the mind's eye of the reader. She may have revered the power of words, marveling at the beauty and truth that stories can command. It may be that these elements all played a part in the motivation to write, but I suspect for Leona it was far more than that. Compelled to write, she hungered to serve God. She found inspiration from the greatest of writings—the Bible. She sensed that writing is eternally important work. Her love for God and his Word, the richness of her devotion, and her gratitude for his salvation and blessings poured forth on the pages she authored.

Leona believed in callings. She personified the teaching in Matthew 5:13–16 to be "salt and light":

> You are the salt of the earth, but if the salt loses its savor, how shall it be seasoned? It is then good for nothing but to be thrown out and trampled underfoot by men. You are the light of the world. A city that is set on a hill cannot be hidden. Nor do they light a lamp and put it under a basket, but on a lampstand, and it gives light to all who are in the house. Let your light so shine before men, that they may see your good works and glorify your Father in heaven. (NKJV)

Leona's manner of living expressed this precept in a unique way: "Be Christ's hands, feet, and heart." Her deep affection for the Word of God shaped all her energy and person. She possessed the "renewed mind" urged upon us all by the Apostle Paul in Romans 12: 1–2:

> I beseech you therefore, brethren, by the mercies of God, that you present your bodies a living sacrifice, holy, acceptable to God, which is your reasonable service. And do not be con-

formed to this world, but be transformed by the
renewing of your mind, that you may prove what
is that good and acceptable and perfect will of
God. (NKJV)

An essential affirmation of the renewed mind is that it seeks
to glorify God above all else, and it desires to see the glory of God
celebrated in the world.

Leona embraced writing and living with her heart sensitive and
receptive, her mind always on the Savior. More than merely creative
expression, she recognized her awakenings as a writer could be used
to instruct, admonish, delight, and transform others and direct them
to the fount of all blessing, Jesus Christ. Her reverence and affection
for God's Word was the bedrock—more than that, the cornerstone—
which moored her life and works. Because first God's Word works in
us, the Holy Spirit works *through* us. As David Mathis tells us, we put
"pen to paper, and fingers to keys."

Ultimately it is a response originating in the writer's deep
inward place, from that parish inhabited by the heart. Spirituality
and humanity in all its fullness—its decorative, lacy fringes; ragged,
torn margins; keen, passionate edges. A writer puts herself and her
thoughts forward for the world to observe and respond. A writer
holds a respect for words and their power to communicate, to stir
genuine connection to deep experience and personal history. Writing
is a place the poet William Stafford called "the realm where miracles
happen." It is a convergence of rivers: the seen on the surface, the
unseen below, lapping at the soul.

"Christ's hands, feet, and heart"—it is a theme abundant in
Leona's letters, universal in the record of her actions. Walking along
the pathways of her life story, there is a vigorous sense of Grandma's
devoted pattern of response: whenever facing a life situation, she
sought to pray, apply God's Word, and then *act*. It is instruction in
living a godly womanly life. This is portrayed gracefully in a short

story Grandma wrote to commemorate and celebrate an important event in any grandma's life—the birth of her first grandchild.

God Gave Gramma an Angel

Leona Moats

I looked down in the same kind of wonder that has filled the hearts of women from the beginning of time, at the tiny pink and white bundle my daughter had laid beside me. So perfect in her creation: hair as soft and white as a cloud, eyes as bright and blue as the sky on a beautiful day in spring. My very first grandchild. So much a replica of her mother. So loved, so cherished, so wanted, so much a gift from God. I held her close wondering how long I'd be able to enjoy this cherished answer to many prayers.

My mind drifted back to the night when, after months of discomfort, I knew that I could no longer prolong the inevitable trip to the doctor. I was sure I had a stomach ulcer but knew that I needed a complete physical.

During a thorough preliminary examination doctor discovered a lump in my breast. Lump, growth, anyway you spell it, the word cancer reared its ugly head. It was decided that further tests were necessary and so arrangements were made.

Suddenly everyday things became important. My cupboards had to be cleaned, the closets cleaned and aired etc. And the happy important things became exceedingly dear. My son would be graduating in a short time. Our first grandchild would be due. Vacation Bible School, where I've had the nursery class for several years, was coming up. I resented this intrusion of illness. I had no time for this interference in my full and happy life.

I went into the hospital…tests, x-rays, dies, more tests. All the time I prayed earnestly and humbly that, God who had never failed me in the past, would find a way to delay things until these things were completed. At last the tests were finished, the results in. By an odd quirk my so called stomach ulcer was, in fact, a rupture in my diaphragm. By choice, I can learn to live with it. The infection in my system could be corrected by treatment and medication. I could, if I wanted to, postpone the biopsy for at least six weeks without too much concern. So it was decided I would go home, thanks to God's intervention.

How long is an eternity? How do you measure it…an hour, a day, a week? It can seem endless. I went back to work. It helped fill the time. My son graduated and I was there with all the other proud parents but I was on borrowed time.

Vacation Bible School was filled with happy days that passed too quickly. I treasured every minute of it. I wanted to hold each dear little one close but they wouldn't have understood.

My borrowed time was running short and still no grandchild. One day I hit a new low in spirit. I went to the only place I know for comfort. The quiet sanctuary of my Lord. Past the point of asking, telling, or wishing, I sat quietly letting the things that were disturbing me run through my mind and quiet tears slid down my cheeks. Suddenly, in the dark recesses of my mind the thought, "Bend thy will to mine." It was as though God was telling me to let him have his way. A peace of mind came over me that I had not known for some time. And I left my worries there with God.

I learned that today was important. Yesterday was gone. It was only important, if I had learned my mistake today, to make it right. Each day must bring a little happiness in someone's life, a card, a visit, a word of cheer or hope. Time could be running out and I must make the most of it. The beloved Twenty Third Psalm continually crept into my mind to comfort and encourage.

At last the long awaited day and now I had my deepest, dearest wish, a tiny grandchild in my arms. They stayed with me for three wonderful days and I savored every minute of it.

After they went home to take up their lives, I sat down and wrote to a cousin, who was slipping away with cancer. The sun was shining through the tiny leaves of spring. The grass had a freshness then, that it doesn't have the rest of the summer. The tulips and iris in my neighbor's yard were a riot of color. If life on earth could be so sweet and beautiful, what then awaited us in heaven? The words of Christ came to me. "In my Father's house are many mansions. I go to prepare a place for you. If it were not so I would tell you." The letter brought comfort to her but it released me also.

Now I could face whatever there was in store for me. How often we build torture chambers in our mind. How many times we let the unknown frighten, even destroy, us, when we have the gift of God's love as close as the prayer in our hearts. God has been gracious and good. He knew that, when he took pity on me and lifted my burden of worries. My fears were unfounded. How can I ever forget the still quiet unspoken voice "Bend thy will to mine."

Each day is precious, yes, but only if it brightens someone else's life.

My little granddaughter is the joy of our lives. Her disposition matches her bright little smile, the soft way she gurgles and coos, the gay little giggle of her mother. She wakes in the morning and plays happily with her feet or watches the fascinating little birds on the side of her bed, quiet and content to wait safe and secure in the love of her parents, knowing in a way we can't fathom that one or the other will be there soon.

My daughter says it frightens her at times. Others have remarked, "She's too perfect to be real." But she is real and God has put his seal of love upon her. For God gave Gramma an Angel.

THE END

Leona's short stories, biographical sketches, and letters reflect the fullness that was her life. Her unpretentious ministry of writing revealed a storehouse of Christlike living. It is a picture of her heart and soul—"Christ's hands and feet"—that compelled the loving acts of faithful service. As years roll on and life's autumn descends on Leona and her family, she assumes the role of matriarch to a large, geographically dispersed clan. While she may not have thought of it this way, the transmission of the discipline and practice of faith is a cultural endeavor delivered from one generation to the next.

The tiny pink-and-white bundle laid in her arms—her first *granddaughter*—grew in grace, love, and faith in the Lord, her grandmother a pillar of strength and an esteemed foremother in the Christian walk of life. Leona's house is the household of faith with a legacy reaching forward to this present day. In a wistful moment, Heidi, that first grandchild, considered the graces gathered in her lifelong relationship with Leona.

Dear Joyce:

Thank you for *all* your efforts! Once you calmed my heart about skeletons, it truly has given me the opportunity to reflect without fear, ponder and even heal. I have often taken the attitude that it is best to let go and let alone—but now you have made it possible to look at the deep waters and know that drowning isn't going to happen. I was blessed through the Lord to have my grandma as a lifeline through her wisdom, encouragement and prayer. How is it—such a person could be surrounded by the most interesting characters? Her insights were never truly available to me until Seth was born. *She* came to stay with me and provided the mentoring I needed to be a mama. She said she never minded those 4 am wake-up calls to nurse her children. She cherished us truly. For *so* many years I looked in the mirror and it was evident I was genetically linked but it wasn't until she came to stay with me I realized where my thought processes came from. No one else in my family shared my sentiment, or understanding of relationships. Our conversations were really special and it was painful to watch her mind disappear as she aged.

Thank you for giving her back to me in a loving way.

Love to you!
Heidi

Later in life, Leona lived with Heidi's family and, in turn, with other granddaughter's families as an alternative to assisted-living care. During these times of residence with Heidi's family, three great-grandchildren came under Leona's watch and care, recipients of the marvelous grace and strength of her presence in their lives. One great-granddaughter, Hannah Wilson, planning to attend college as an English major and author, wrote a college application essay interpreting Leona's relationship and influence in her life:

> Her hair is the color of snow; her eyes a dim blue, hidden behind glasses. She is nearly ninety years old, and uses a walker to get from place to place, stopping to catch her breath for long intervals at a time. Walking through the grocery store, she asks a question for a third time. At the answer, her wrinkled face twists in confusion. A passerby moves over slightly and continues talking on his phone as she hobbles down the aisle. As she leaves the grocery store, the man in front of her does not hold the door. Her granddaughter, however, races ahead to keep it open so she can walk through. This woman seems lost and bewildered, asking again if the time on her watch is correct. Her questions and slow shuffle are irritating and the cause of much impatience to others like the store clerks. It would be easy to ignore or disregard this great-grandmother of eighteen, leaving her to be lost in memories or the repetitive thoughts of the present, but I don't want to. She is my great-grandmother, Leona

Moats, a woman who hasn't wasted a day in her life. She has lived each day to the fullest, working hard and extending herself to others. Even as she gets older, my grandma still gives freely and loves openly, and this is her legacy.

While it might seem that she is a hindrance, getting in the way of my family's social functions, I see her as a blessing and a part of our community. The activities and events she is a part of are transformed into letters of encouragement to those in need. For the past forty years, Grandma has written to about thirty people each week. Being in our lives allows her to share the wisdom she has treasured up over the years. She isn't ignored or overlooked like she would be in a nursing home. Instead, she is welcomed and included. After volleyball games, my friends have hugged her and asked how she was doing. At church she can always be found praying with a fellow worshipper. Grandma might be slow in arriving to her seat, but she is quick to reach out to those around her.

Although Grandma is hardly capable of making her own breakfast of eggs and toast, she isn't any less accomplished. She began work at the age of twelve, washing dishes for twenty-five cents a day. Then, ultimately to care for her family, she began entry level work on the night shift at Kellogg's as a garbage collector. When she retired after thirty-two years, she was working in the lab with chemical engineers. She only had an eleventh grade education. Currently, Grandma is fighting against becoming completely dependent on the aid of others. She might be limited, but she still does what she can. She is not able to cook dinner, but she helps set the table. She can't clean the house, but she folds the laundry. At almost ninety she is not in a wheelchair waiting for something to do, instead she is right beside the family, working and involved.

Even in her forgetfulness, Grandma is a source of wisdom and strength for me. Her life stories show her determination and passion for living. She has been my inspiration, not letting the lack of a high school diploma or a college education get in the way of her success. When I look at my grandma, I see a woman of benevolence with laughing eyes, an impish grin, and a listening ear. She might use her walker and repeat herself, but she doesn't give up. She loves those around her and makes it known. Her letters and prayers are full of understanding and humility. In the years that she has stayed with us, people have tried to push her away and out of life, commenting on all the hard work we have to do. With our help, however, she pushes back, determined not to be beaten down by the world. She doesn't want to finish her life sitting in a room by herself. So, each morning when I bring her breakfast, and she looks up at me and quietly says, "Thank you," I look down at her and think, "No Grandma, thank you."

Hannah Wilson
William Jewell Application Essay

Like Leona, school was for me a great influence in developing my literate life. Reading and writing were favorite subjects well taught by good teachers. Writing assignments for English class were the easiest of homework. Given the choice between writing an essay and doing a speech for class, I took the writing assignment every time. To my surprise, I received great encouragement from my teachers. Twelfth-grade English teacher Dorothy Perry submitted a piece of my writing from a creative writing assignment to a contest sponsored by Lawrence Institute of Technology, a local four-year university. I won. The legacy of this splendid instruction is a lifelong love of nonfiction reading and, of course, writing.

But the credit for these interests and abilities harkens back to subtle, powerful influences hardly ever recognized at the time; they become apparent and appreciated through the lens of reflection. I now know the creative act and expression of writing was somehow absorbed from my mother. As a child, I remember rounding the corner into the kitchen, seeing her silhouette in the window by the kitchen table, writing a letter to her bachelor brothers in the old home place in Pennsylvania. She wrote letters to my uncles in faraway parts of the country; she wrote letters to my aunts who lived twenty miles away in Detroit. Long-distance telephone calls were too expensive in the 1960s. Some of those letters survive. I found them in a tattered, disintegrating box bound with rubber bands, the dust from the paper an acrid bitterness to the senses. It was one of the few heirlooms worth salvaging from my old home place.

As children do, we discovered that our mother was holding out on us, and then we discovered where. Deep in a file-folder-sized kitchen drawer in a brown envelope, she stored her inspirations and her own writings, creative pieces clipped from newspapers, short articles from *Reader's Digest*, quotes and sayings, poems, her own poetry. Almost all her poems were rhyming poetry in even-numbered stanzas. From time to time when she was at work, I pulled out the drawer, removing the folder, running my eyes over her fine, even handwritten pages, seeking discoveries of hidden family life and of my mother's life.

My mother hid her writing in a drawer. Leona put her writing forward into the world to bless others and to proclaim Christ.

A legacy is at least in part what someone leaves behind for future generations. Writing about a legacy invites others into the sanctuary of deepest experiences, the wisdom, challenges, love, hope, and blessings of this life. Grandma intended her writing to comfort others and to be a witness to her journey of faith. She knew instinctively to instill for posterity what she held to be most true, most dear, and most decisive in her life—loving God with all her heart, soul, mind, and strength and loving her neighbor. Her intent in it all was to glorify her Lord and Savior Jesus.

I once wondered, as an outsider to this astonishing story, if it mattered that I was not "family." Through God's merciful providential care I learn about being a part of the family of God by adoption into Leona's life and kinsfolk. The Lord of the universe directs, provides, and cares for his people. He preserves us on our life's journey, employing his own heavenly family to do the job. He provides for me all the days of my life. Among those acts of mercy and care, He brought Leona to me—a guide, counselor, teacher, comforter, friend, "Christ's hands, feet, and heart."

Now I know it never mattered at all.

CHAPTER 5

Work on the Night Shift

Kellogg's Factory Omaha, Nebraska 1980

She began her career sweeping floors and emptying wastebaskets. She retired as a salaried employee and supervisor in the chemistry laboratory, working alongside highly educated engineers. She was responsible for the experiments, data collection, and scientific work essential to create high-quality cereal products, and she had a pension to boot. The Kellogg's Company in Omaha, Nebraska, became part of Leona's life for the next thirty years.

By 1947, Leona and Ronald had established a home in Council Bluffs. Daughter Sandy was seven, and son Richard was three. Ronald worked for the Union Pacific Railroad. The family attended Dodge Memorial Congregational Church, a stone's throw across the alley from their house at 2301 Avenue G. Leona sought a job at one of the newest employers in the Council Bluffs area—Kellogg's Company. With a growing family's needs, she wanted to work long enough to buy a washer and a dryer.

Kellogg's, headquartered in Battle Creek, Michigan, opened the second plant in its history in 1942 in Omaha, Nebraska, just across the Missouri River from Council Bluffs. Omaha shared the rich frontier heritage of Council Bluffs, and together the sister cities became the Midwest's most powerful hub for transportation, materials, and services for the robust westward expansion of our country. Lands west of the Missouri River opened to settlement after the passage of the Kansas-Nebraska Act of 1854. The rugged and rough-edged town of Omaha incorporated in 1857, and in 1862, Congress passed the Pacific Railway Act. President Abraham Lincoln declared Omaha the eastern terminus of the Transcontinental Railroad in December 1863, and this prescient act inaugurated the growth of the Omaha area. In time, Omaha became a supply depot for rail distribution of goods to settlers throughout the western states. By 1893, the largest stockyards in the US would do business in Omaha, stimulating development no doubt attractive to companies like Kellogg's. Situated at the edge of the vast farmlands and prairies of the Great Plains, the newest Kellogg's plant was perfectly positioned for the procurement of raw materials—corn and wheat—the use of available rail transportation to deliver products to the tables of hungry people, and the access to the labor force necessary to produce them.

But in 1942, World War II was on. Manufacturing companies throughout the United States refocused production efforts to support the war effort. The Kellogg Company had a reputation in the food industry, well-earned by the values and principles of its founder W. K. Kellogg, particularly in the field of nutrition. Mary I. Barber, head of the home economics department at Kellogg's and president of the American Dietetic Association, was called from her job at the company to be "on loan" as food consultant to the US quartermaster general. She designed the nutritional standards and menus used to produce food for the US Army. Kellogg's also produced "K Rations" for the US military. Developed to replace heavier, cumbersome C rations, "K Rats" were boxed meals served as breakfast, dinner, and supper units. A "breakfast" meal consisted of canned meat product, biscuits, compressed cereal bar, powdered coffee, fruit bar, chewing gum, sugar tablets, four cigarettes, water-purification tablets, a can opener, and a wooden spoon. Dinner and supper units were composed of similar elements. More than 105 million of these rations were produced, feeding troops in the European and Pacific theaters of the war. Under Barber's leadership, Kellogg's also developed a "Food for Victory" program for civilians, which offered food preparation classes and distributed recipes that used nonrationed food available to homemakers. Kellogg's Company spent nearly $200,000 in the 1940s on this program, work which earned it the Army-Navy "E" flag for excellence. The government called upon businesses to stretch every physical asset in service to the war effort. Not to be outdone by the food department, Kellogg's engineers even converted the new machine shop at the Omaha plant to manufacture parts and supplies for the US military including components for the top-secret Manhattan Project.

By 1947, when Leona joined the company, Kellogg's returned to prewar activities of new product development and distribution to a country eager to throw off the shortages and sacrifices of the war years. W. K. Kellogg remained at the helm of the company, now vastly different from the little laboratory at the Battle Creek Sanitarium in the early 1900s where the first product known as cereal was made.

Will Keith Kellogg, born in 1860 in Battle Creek, Michigan, and who was the younger brother of Dr. John Harvey Kellogg, quit school after completing a sixth-grade education. He went to work, drifting through a variety of low-skills jobs including that of selling brooms for his father's broom factory. In 1880 he was hired by Dr. John Harvey Kellogg at the Western Health Reform Institute in Battle Creek as a bookkeeper by day and foods experimenter at all other times.

Battle Creek in the 1860s was a community on the frontier of the United States, a destination for settlers from New England streaming westward. This movement was more than a manner of settling the land, building homes, and raising families. Freedom of religious practice was at least as powerful and important in the migration as was creating one's own homestead. The Battle Creek area became a thriving settlement and center for the operations of the Seventh-day Adventist Church, of which the Kellogg family was an early and principal part.

Ellen G. White and her husband, James White, were influential figures in the seventh-day movement emerging from its roots in the Second Great Awakening and Millerism. The Second Great Awakening developed from the work of Bible societies in the early 1800s, making affordable Bibles available to those who wished to study the Scriptures on their own. The unforeseen result of this egalitarian effort was the formation of various religious minority movements and groups, among them the Millerite Movement, stepping away from mainline churches and orthodox theology. When the movement's prediction of the second advent of Christ on October 22, 1844, failed to materialize, disillusioned Millerite churches and followers still sought to continue the study of prophesy and Bible truths. Leaders from these churches began "Sabbath conferences" to discuss doctrinal issues, one of them a peculiarly contentious issue of a seventh-day Sabbath. Between 1848 and 1850, twenty-two conferences were held in New England and New York. By 1860, with growth among the congregations, delegates from Adventist groups met and decided to name the organization Seventh-day Adventists. In 1863, the first general conference of Seventh-day Adventists formalized the denomination. Prominent among the organizers of the conferences were Hiram Edson, Joseph Bates, James Springer White, and Ellen G. White. These early organizers of the Seventh-day Adventist Church were persuasive in shaping the church's focus in two main areas: missionary efforts and medical work.

Now Ellen G. White was a receiver of visions, holder of the gift of prophesy. She claimed to receive over two thousand visions during her lifetime. In 1849, White was convinced in a vision that her husband should publish a newspaper. Titled *The Present Truth*, it was at first distributed to friends and others interested in the work. Publishing became an important part of the missionary and revival work that created momentum crucial to the cause. White wrote profusely, composing her first book in 1851 and eventually publishing over five thousand articles and forty books in her lifetime. Increasing demand and interest in her writings strained the homespun handpress publishing house in Rochester, New York, the Whites' headquarters.

Missionary zeal and the magnetic draw of the West kept the early leaders on the move. Joseph Bates, while visiting Jackson, Michigan, in 1852, had a dream about sailing into a port named Battle Creek. Propelled by this epiphany, he traveled north and west to Battle Creek and formed a small worshiping community there. In 1855, the Battle Creek Seventh-day Adventist believers invited the Whites and their printing business to relocate there, promising to provide a building and offices, and Battle Creek blossomed into the center of Seventh-day Adventist activities for years to come.

Ellen G. White maintained her writing ministry throughout her life, and now with the incipient support of the church in Battle Creek, she turned to other visionary matters. In 1863, she received a vision of the relation of physical health to spirituality: the benefits of sunshine, clean air, pure water, and exercise in the care of the body leading to a vessel fit for the care of the soul. She reported this vision at the June 1863 general conference and convinced church leadership that an emphasis on good health practices should be part of the healing and missions activity of the church. A health education program was begun and a publications series produced. As this mission work gained acceptance, plans were laid in 1866 for a health institute to provide health instruction and care for the sick. Thus was born the Western Health Reform Institute in Battle Creek.

The rudimentary program had its rustic beginnings in a two-story farmhouse just outside Battle Creek. During the first ten years, the enterprise struggled to gain public confidence in its therapies: sunshine, water, rest, exercise, a vegetarian diet, and abstention from alcohol, coffee, and animal flesh. The Western Health Reform Institute came close to financial ruin. In 1876, however, the hiring of Dr. John Harvey Kellogg proved to be the turning point for the Institute's survival and for its eventual prosperity.

John Harvey Kellogg's family was among the original Adventist group organized by Joseph Bates in 1855. One of seventeen children, he and his siblings had little public schooling—deemed unnecessary, for the day of the Lord was expected imminently—but nevertheless he acquired a self-taught education through voracious reading. He was hired by the Whites to work in the printing business, where his prodigious intellect did not go unnoticed. Kellogg yearned to be a teacher, but the Whites convinced him and sponsored him to take a six-month-long medical course at the Hygeio-Therapeutic College in New Jersey. Inspired by this training and with the Whites' support, he attended medical school at the University Medical School in Ann Arbor, Michigan, and at New York Medical College in New York City, graduating in 1875 with a medical degree. In 1876, he hired on as the medical director of the Western Health Reform Institute. Apparently taking charge immediately, in 1877, he renamed it the Battle Creek Medical Surgical Sanitarium.

Kellogg embraced the Adventist health precepts and wrote extensively on vegetarianism. The "San," as it became known, had an experimental kitchen through which a "school of cookery" held classes and published cookbooks. Food, to Dr. Kellogg, was a powerful therapeutic especially if it was soft to chew and easy to digest. His experiments with breakfast foods began shortly after his arrival at the San and eventually involved his wife and younger brother, Will Keith Kellogg.

Will Keith Kellogg also had little formal schooling and at the age of fourteen went to work at his father's broom factory in Battle Creek. Disdaining the life of a traveling salesman and peddler, he accepted a job offer from his brother, John Harvey, to be a bookkeeper and general handyman at the San. The stage was set for the collaboration that would lead to the development of flaked cereal.

Dr. John Harvey Kellogg worked for years with a recipe for ground grains and toasted dough that would later become known as granola. But in 1894, the Kellogg brothers also experimented with a dough made from wheat berries. A batch was made one evening, but Dr. Kellogg was unexpectedly called away, and the dough was forgotten until the next morning. The dough softened; this "tempering" was important in the next brilliantly developed step. Being thrifty and not wanting to discard the dough, the brothers rolled it into thin sheets, baked it, then flaked it. Later, the same process was used to process rice then corn. The cornflake was born.

This delicious, toasty, tasty food was a "hit" with the patients at the San. Dr. John Harvey patented the product in 1896, selling it through the Sanitas Food Company, his health-foods enterprise. But John Harvey was willing to share his discoveries about food, allowing visitors and even patients at the San to observe his processes. One observer, a patient at the San in 1891, was a man named C. W. Post. He went on to create his own health foods company in 1892, eventually developing a product in direct competition with Kellogg's cornflakes. This brought to a head a disagreement between John Harvey and Will Keith. Recognizing the commercial and business potential of flaked cereal products, Will Keith stepped out on his own, forming the Battle Creek Toasted Corn Flakes Company in 1906. More than one hundred years later, "K-e-double l-o-double g" Kellogg's Company, still serves a worldwide market with "wholesome cereal foods" for everyone, not just those with special health or dietary needs.

All of our lives are part of history. When a job became available at Kellogg's that relieved Leona of the drudgery of janitorial work, she stepped into a position "on the belt." Workers wore white smocks and caps and stood alongside the conveyor belts, carrying cereal on its way to packaging. Burned or misshapen cereal was scraped from the belt, an early form of quality control. Some workers helped themselves to cereal snacks along the way. Leona's wage was sixty-eight cents per hour. For a time, payday included a free box of cereal.

Leona worked her way up to night supervisor on the line, novel at the time since most supervisory personnel were male. She settled into the night shift for twenty-one years and somewhere in this time frame gained a promotion to Mary I. Barber's testing laboratory. There she took up a position in charge of the testing and experiments in the chemistry laboratory, a woman with an eleventh-grade education working shoulder to shoulder with men who had engineering degrees. Family legend tells us that she had no confidence in her abilities, but the record of her movement to jobs with greater responsibility gives away the fact that she was very smart and was valued by others for her ability to solve problems. Granddaughter Heidi relates two stories:

> A male colleague with an engineering degree was looking over her calculations one day and asked her where she had learned "new math." She did not understand what he was asking of her, to be honest. She told me she prayed over everything she did while she worked. He told her that whatever the case, the way she was calculating was "new math." I got the impression it was a condescending comment rather than admiration.
>
> She told me about another time when she was totally in charge of the lab. She said it was a very frightening situation for her because she had to do all the chemistry experiments required and they would be compared to the outcomes of the lab in Battle Creek. When the arduous tasks were completed EVERY single experiment came out EXACTLY as the experiments in Battle Creek. She prayed over every experiment, every calculation.

So she walked with the Lord and carried his presence with her wherever her work responsibilities lay. That focus—her love for the Savior—remained the eminent purpose in her life. She developed many personal relationships during her workaday life, nurtured in prayer groups and Bible studies during lunch breaks. The "middle of the night" counted for Christ, as she explains.

> It's the middle of the night. My time to be alone with God. I worked the night shift for twenty-one years. It afforded the time to pick up on the prayers others offered in the day time. Often

in the night I find myself seeking the company of my Lord and bringing to him those concerns for friends, for family. For concerns on the Prayer Chain as I feel led by the Spirit. Or just to earnestly seek the Lord for someone his Spirit may lay on my heart. When I worked I often promised to pray someone through the night and did.

Returning home in the early morning from the "night shift," Leona often made a stop at a neighbor's house just across the alley from her home in Council Bluffs. It was a friendship that would last more than forty years and is recalled with much fondness by this friend, Ann Tholen.

Ann would invite her in for a morning cup of coffee. Leona would sit down with the heaviness of someone who had been on her feet all night and "dust the Kellogg's sugar off her glasses." Leona was, in Ann's words,

> Like a sister to me. She was 10 years older than I. Those were fun times, family activities, women's groups things, prayer times. For years we got together in the fall for salsa-making parties. I grew up in the Nazarene church, a very conservative church, very legalistic—live by the law. I had fallen away from the church, and in some ways from faith. Leona never preached to me. But she was the one who brought me back, to God and to the church. I started going to church at Dodge Memorial, Leona's church. To me, the church was more secular, but very loving people. It was about this time that Leona and Ron moved from Council Bluffs north about 30 miles to Honey Creek, but they still attended Dodge Memorial. In the mid-1990's after Ron's death, she moved back to Council Bluffs. Dodge Memorial had declined to about 10 members, so

we began going to service at a Nazarene church. This church had singers and a choir, and a young pastor who was a good preacher. Those were good times. And I miss her so.

Ann Tholen lives in the Council Bluffs area, and now the "service" and hymn singers from this church come to the retirement community in which she resides.

We are all a part of history. Leona wrote with a sense of leaving a legacy, speaking to the life we are called to inhabit in Christ—to be "His hands, feet, and heart." She believed God's grace had been poured out upon her, and it became a vital part of her living to channel that to others. She believed in being ready at a moment's notice in prayer, having a "kingdom zeal" for others in need. It was a way to thank God for his faithfulness and celebrate his providential care. It is an expression of our own hearts renewed in God's image, enabling us to have compassion and to act in mercy toward others. We do so out of grateful obedience to God, who first extended his mercy and kindness to us.

Leona's legacy also reflects the invisible thread of connections across generations, for those in her family who influenced her and came before her and now for those who have come after. Her writings are that record. Her history is an endowment of inspiration, the past unrolled for our understanding, the expectation that we should become sensitive to God's leading to shape our future service for him. The history and legacy of Leona's faith is something to take into our own history, our faith, and our influence in the world.

So we pray for others. Bring heartfelt concerns to our Lord. Share our praise and thanksgiving. Weep for the grace and mercy to fall on our concerns for those whose health has failed, for hearts that are broken, lives suddenly brought to grief. Ask God for wisdom for those making decisions. My prayers have been for many things and people this night. But once the Lord said in

Jeremiah 32:27, "Behold: I am the Lord, the God of all flesh: is there anything too hard for me?"

We can add our amen to this, for surely we have all seen and experienced his grace and mercy and found a strength or help beyond ourselves and come to realize his eye is on the sparrow and I know he is watching over me and those I bring to him.

Leona Moats, Contestant for "Sweetheart Queen of Kellogg's Corn Crop 1956"

CHAPTER 6

The Common and the Uncommon

Screenhouse for Writing at Honey Creek

Pastor Jeff is waiting at the entry doors as I enter the church. "I have something for you. Heidi brought it back with her from her trip to Omaha." In his hands rests a white binder, at least three inches thick, bulky, substantial. He seems relieved to deliver it my way. I will soon learn the value of the trove placed in my hands. It is a collection of Leona's letters, which she sent to one dear sister in Christ more than twenty years ago.

Leona made friends easily, cared for them ardently, kept them as precious gems. As time went on and she moved to different homes throughout the Plains states, the connections forged in sundry communities and churches were kept intact through her weekly letters to her friends. Over a thirty-year letter writing ministry, her mailing list grew to more than forty recipients.

Tucked away in the collected family archives of scrapbooks and photo albums resided this large white notebook. Heidi's sister Amy in Omaha came across it while cleaning a closet and thought I might like to browse its contents. Heidi dutifully loaded it into carryon luggage for the plane ride home.

From the moment I opened the binder cover, I sensed the special nature of this object—an artifact, an heirloom. It had been carefully curated. Here were 388 letters collected by a treasured friend in Omaha who traveled life's pathways with Leona. As the letters arrived over the years, they are carefully stored in the binder, three-hole punched, smooth and flat. The letters are addressed to "Sally and Ray," but other than first names, no one now recalls where Leona befriended them. Upon Sally's passing, her daughter Cindy returned the letters and binder to Leona's family with a loving and lasting tribute letter of her own.

> Dearest Leona:
>
> Here is the "Leona Bible" that mom referred to—
>
> I stopped in to see Dad this weekend and came across your note in a sympathy card. Mom had intended to give this back to you. As you can see, she had written in the front of this. I was going to put your pages in a bigger binder, but thought better of it after I found the handwritten note in the front of this one.
>
> As I read through many of your inspirational notes, it reminds me of passages from cards by Helen Steiner Rice—you could publish some

of these! I know God works in very mysterious, yet loving ways. You truly have a 'gift,' Leona. I know you inspired my mother through your loving ways and, of course, your written words.

Our relative, Howard, is a priest in the catholic church I believe in Harlan, Iowa. He said it best at mom's funeral. He spoke of how much deeper her faith in the Lord became as she depended on him in her battle with cancer. It's true—she certainly did put her trust in God to see her through, and she was such an inspiration and comfort to others who were experiencing very similar conditions in their cancer struggle.

So Leona I didn't make copies of your words—these are the "originals" that mom had. I'm hoping that a small part of the joy and pleasure that mom found in reading these and feeling the love, will come back threefold to your granddaughter, Amy. God bless her and her three little ones. Also, God bless her husband as he serves in the Air Force. Particularly God bless you, Leona for using the gift God has given you in writing—you are a blessed soul. I know my mom so appreciated your words and friendship. The reunion with her in heaven will give us great joy and exhilaration one day!

Sally's daughter,
Cindy Fitzgerald

Three hundred eighty-eight letters lovingly kept. This is more than three times my collection of 106 letters and, taken as a weekly production, spans more than seven years. It is a rich reserve, a rare and fortunate window into one woman's Christian walk driven by a love for the Lord and for the written word. The realization dawns: did Leona have any idea of the value this collection might bear? Did she dare hope that perhaps someday there might indeed be a book-length anthology of the text? I have the prickly feeling writers get when presented with an endeavor worthy of attention. The window shade flutters open onto Leona's writing life.

Leona's two-page letters appear at first glance to be related to the genre of journals. Since antiquity, people have had the urge to record thoughts, ideas, and sentiments. The record of journaling—its history—extends back to early civilizations. Archaeologists have uncovered rare archives of daily life similar to accounting ledgers, the annals of public economic and social life. Journaling persevered through time and prospered with the improvement of materials—paper and writing tools—and the emergence and place of education in society. Daily journals began to develop the characteristics familiar to us today: a place to annotate and explore ideas; a place to reflect, write, and work through matters of importance, figure things out; a place to express anxieties, worries, and frustrations. In our present time, some contemporary specialized journals such as the *Gratitude Journal* turn hearts to positive elements in everyday life and create a therapeutic space. In the ever-increasing speed of daily life, the technique of the "bullet journal" wedges its way into the time-strapped millennial's writing practice. The educator in me sighs; at least they're writing. For many of us, our first experience in the crafting of expressive, organized writing occurred as we were taught the fundamentals in our school experiences. But with great good fortune, this academic act broke free from its scholastic boundaries.

Imagine an afternoon at the family homestead, upstairs in the attic, sorting through the grandparents' steamer trunk and finding a sheaf of love letters tied with a frayed red ribbon. More discoveries await: opening a box of faded postcards commemorating a honeymoon world trip; a passel of telegrams bound in a folio, embossed with an ornate monogram; or a gilt-edged book, leather-bound, crumbling, with bruised corners, filled with pages of neat, Palmer-method india ink script. Journaling takes its place among so many different ways to record, reflect, and explore ideas as they unfold.

But personal forms of writing—letters, postcards, telegrams, today's forms of electronic writing—are personal. I am convinced

Leona's letters carry journaling to a different level, to a higher focus and intent.

In some forms of educational practice, young scholars keep copybooks. The copybook becomes a place where the student copies quotes or portions of literature which seem interesting or worth remembering, gleaned from reading or engagement with books. The learned practice and discipline of looking for beautiful literature passages and comely language patterns imprints the developing minds and hearts. The student begins the lifelong training of the habits of the literate mind, the most valuable of which is attentive reading—paying attention to and actively looking for influential and worthy passages of texts. Over time, with much diligence and practice, writing down inspiring, noteworthy, and impressionable texts enriches thinking, writing, and other creative work. The rewards for such work include the virtue of wisdom and, as noted by philosopher Brand Blandshard, "ideals and aspirations that a spirit lives by."

Eventually the practice of journals or copybooks became the art of commonplacing. Beyond the privacy implied in journals, commonplacing moves up a level in sophistication, providing the structure and disciplined reflection to be used in purposeful, creative writing. Roman and Greek philosophers practiced commonplacing, the most notable of which is Marcus Aurelius, whose *Meditations* from the second century remains the benchmark of modern works. He quotes portions of works by the Athenian playwright Aristophanes and from other tragedies and plays of Euripides and Sophocles. He records memorable works of poets and philosophers: Epicurus, Plato, Pindar. It is sometimes said you are the company you keep, and the author of a commonplace book has complete control over the quality of that which is transcribed, shaping the intellectual world in which he travels. Marcus Aurelius set the standards high. By the seventeenth century, commonplacing is taught as a formal practice in classical rhetoric training and scholastic work. The tradition makes its way into the world in the intellectual life and study discipline of philosophers, scientists, and theologians—anyone of the rational and scholarly guilds.

Benjamin Franklin kept a commonplace book where he tracked progress on his self-improvement program of living his Thirteen Virtues. So did Thomas Jefferson and Ludwig von Beethoven. Thomas Edison's writings were scribed in his Private Ideas Book. Mark Twain, W. H. Auden, Madeleine L'Engle, and H. L. Mencken cultivated creative inspiration in commonplace books. Virginia Woolf spent deliberate time in her commonplace book, "trying out the art of writing." Among statesmen, Ronald Reagan is well known for his commonplace book which took the form of a precisely arranged card file of anecdotes, stories, and aphorisms. Having his favorite thoughts and opinions conveniently available made life easier for his speechwriters. One of the most fascinating, extensive collections of commonplace books are those of Leonardo Da Vinci, who produced at least fifty of them, some 25,000 pages of drawings and text on art, painting, engineering, philosophy, architecture, theories and inventions, and on anything, apparently, that interested him. But perhaps the most compelling modern commonplace book remains that of Anne Frank, whose diary became part therapeutic tool, part confidant, part intentional archive to document the extraordinary experiences of her time. She may have had future readers in mind. In it is recorded an enigmatic observation—"Paper has more patience than people."

So Leona stands in the grand tradition of men and women "of letters" though she would never have called herself by such a highbrow title. It is a profound gift to see this set of letters as a whole, its own form of literature, powerful, persuasive, emanating its life and light. My spirit is quickened by the richness of her exhortations, the grace of the unadorned workings of a life of faith, repentant, reverent, holy. This she spreads as a feast before her readers then and now.

As often as possible, Leona spends early mornings in the screenhouse of her home, in the trailer beside the Missouri River north of Council Bluffs, greeting day and the awakening of nature, turning her heart in prayer and praise to God. She loves the first tawny notes of birdsong, the stirrings of small animals, the soft mirror of sunrise and its gauzy cloak over her country landscape. She sets pen to paper, her inspiration the Word of God. She usually begins with a story or an anecdote, something going on in her life, her family's life, a friend's life. Sometimes it is an observation on an event occurring in the world. At times, she begins with a cascade of hymns or Scripture quotes. The "loves" of her life—family, people, nature—are the background canvas.

This triggers a remembered Scripture or Bible story which kindles her musings. She takes a theme from this scripture which resonates in her heart and mind and walks with it—taking the reader along to share the reality of her communion with God; her wonder and thankfulness for his presence and grace in her life; the comfort and security shed abroad in her soul; learning what to value in life; the wholeness, satisfaction, and completeness of her experience with the Lord.

As time is passing, Leona is ever more intent on reviewing her life and on testifying to God's goodness toward her. There is much thankfulness for all the good things provided but also a reckoning of the time spent in "God's woodshed." She cherishes just plain people especially her family. Laughter and love fill her house when her family gathers for the holidays, and they come from all over the country. She maintained a lively interest and ability to enjoy the world through travel and activities, always seeing God's hand at work and giving thanks for his gracious provision. God's merciful sustaining grace in times of trouble and heartache are the other side of the blessed joys— the building of the Christlike qualities of patience and endurance. She has learned to be a comforter, encouraging and supporting others. She ends her writing, exactly two pages, by employing a simple technique that swings the reader back to the opening story, adding a reflection or two and a closing exhortation to turn to the Lord and receive his blessings.

With the surprising combination of the realm of nature with the routine of housework, Leona convinces us that even these belong together in giving thanks to the Lord.

Dear Sally:

We enjoyed a couple of truly spring like days. I even washed some of my windows. It seemed so good to be able to open them and let the fresh air in. This spring fever just hasn't gone away. Still it is a good feeling to see the floor in my closet and the shelves in order. Or have the sun stream through clean windows. Sometimes the Lord has to clean the windows of my soul to help me remember I have more to be thankful for than sorry about. It makes me aware of how blessed I am when I see my troubles through his eyes. Then I can honestly say I'm just fine for the shape I'm in. No wonder Psalm 46:10 says, Be still and know that I am God. It puts a whole new perspective on situations we think are beyond us or our abilities. Then God can be glorified and we can feel his presence in our life. One of the joys I look forward to when I get to heaven is to sit at his feet and just enjoy him forever.

In Leona's world, the reality of her faith is the complete companion informing every event in her life. She applies the truth of the Gospel to everything. Faith is strengthened through the trials we experience along the way. If God by his marvelous providence sets before her an opportunity to testify to his mercy and grace in one of those experiences, she accepts the mission.

Brought to mind is a time in my life when I was physically and emotionally drained over a surgery. One day I quit asking, I just sat quietly in the sanctuary (at church) and the still small voice of God spoke. "Accept this thing for my sake." Such peace poured over me. Nothing had changed outwardly. But inside of me had. I went to the hospital. Was put in a room with a young black woman. That didn't happen in those days. She pulled the curtain between us. But she soon discovered we loved the same Lord. She was a young mother with several children. She was fearful of the surgery. The future. For her children. We began to share scripture. Sing. Prayer. When my minister came he was surprised to find us having a hallelujah time. Mine was benign. But hers would require treatment. Yet her fear was gone, and she knew God was very present in all this.

Among the most striking and comely aspects of Leona's life is the high value she places on experiencing the nearness of the Lord. This thirst for his presence is cultivated through continued meditation upon his Word.

My children got home Thursday evening and the place came alive. Dinner was ready. I baked a peach pie. I had frozen some Colorado peaches ahead of time. We love our families and like to make special preparations for them when we know they are coming. I like to think the Lord makes special preparations to welcome us home. What a day that will be.

But this is the here and now and we must live the gift of each day. One of the most beautiful Psalms is Psalm 100. Surely this one lends itself to putting the thanks back into Thanksgiving.

We lived across the alley from the church we attended. Raising children in those days revolved around church and school. Praise the Lord even their social life was there. How thankful I am for the Sunday School teachers who helped to shape their lives spiritually and with moral values. Verse

2 of Psalm 100 says, Serve the Lord with gladness, come before His presence with singing. For me there was a special sense of God's presence in the quiet beauty of the sanctuary there.

Verse 3: Know that the Lord He is God, it is He that made us and not we ourselves, we are His people and the sheep of His pasture. When this Psalm was written the shepherd's care of his flock was very personal. They led their sheep to good feeding grounds. Protected them from wild animals. Used the crook of their staff to rescue a lamb that might have lost its footing on narrow paths.

I took a good look at that verse and thought how God shaped my life from the time I received him as Lord and Savior. Looking back it is a blessing to remember the people who came into my life. People who taught me the Word of God. Who shared my love for the Lord. Those who prayed with me and for me. When life presented problems too big for me, I could slip into the church and pray. The beauty and peace of the sanctuary never failed to lend itself to soothing the troubled waters. I would go home feeling the peace only God could give. How comforting to know we are his people and indeed the sheep of his pasture. Verse 4: Enter into His gates with thanksgiving and into His courts with praise; be thankful unto Him and bless His name.

Sometimes his goodness and mercy overwhelms me and turns my prayers just to thanking God for who he is. Finding comfort in knowing God knows me better than I know myself and he loves me. What an awesome thought that is. I find myself saying Oh Father, forgive me. Mold me. Shape me into what You want me to

be. I love you so much. Thank you for loving me.
How comforting are the words of Jesus in John
15:16: Ye have not chosen Me, but I have chosen
you. Joy leaps in my heart. God loves me! May
that joy fill you too.

Such meditation fills her life and reflects that which Paul says in
Acts 17:28: In Him we live and move and have our being (NKJV.)

Scripture and hymns blend together in her meditations and
preparations for writing, an expression of the thankfulness by which
Leona lives. She loves spiritual songs and used them with reverence,
in the manner of commonplacing, to help the reader picture the joy
in her soul.

When we walk with the Lord. In the light
of his word. What a glory he sheds on our way.
While we do his good will. He abides with us
still. And with all who will trust and obey.

Those beautiful words floated through my
thoughts when I sat down to write. It was Sunday
evening. My favorite day of the week. To enter
into it realizing this is the day the Lord hath
made, I will rejoice and be glad in it. The antici-
pation of entering his gates. Of sharing his word.
Of singing his praise. Of sharing what God has
done or is doing in our life or in those who gather
with us is joy unspeakable.

The teacher asked us today (in Sunday
School) if we could remember a particular time
of joy in our lives. I remembered a time when
the Billy Graham Crusade came to Omaha. I was
working as a Counselor (at the meetings.) I did
not know that my son came to the meeting. At
the Invitation he had gone forward and accepted
Christ. We train up our children to love the
Lord. But the rubber meets the road when they

make their own profession of faith. My friend was also helping that night, and she had the good fortune of seeing the card he had signed. She was his Sunday School teacher. So for both of us you could say, we knew the meaning of joy unspeakable.

Leona's topics for her letters cover a surprising range. She muses freely and forthrightly on the Christian's experience in suffering, obedience, and submission. We endure and serve because of Christ's work for us. How interesting it would have been to sit in on this Sunday School class discussion.

> We've been studying evangelism. Our scripture was 1 Peter 3:15: But in your hearts set apart Christ as Lord. Always be prepared to give an answer to everyone who asks you to give the reason for the hope you have. I could never walk up to someone, as a granddaughter does, and ask, Do you know Jesus as your savior? But we are told in Matthew 28:19, Go into the world and teach, baptizing them in the name of the Father and Son and Holy Ghost. So we are asked to tell what Jesus did for us. I've a lifetime of experiences to draw from. Our teacher asks why are we allowed to suffer? In my mind I recall Hebrews 5:8: Though He were a son, yet learned He obedience through the things He suffered.
>
> When you think of what obedience cost Jesus, who are we to question why God allows us to go through trials? Yes and even suffer. But Jesus looked beyond the suffering and saw the glory before him and knew he would sit down at the right hand of the Majesty on high (Hebrews 1:3.) A very dear woman spoke up. Reminding us everyone has sinned. Some more than others.

But she reminded us Jesus paid for all sins. He assured us of our place in heaven with him. We need not relive our guilt. We have become a new creature in Christ (2Corinthians 5:17.)

I don't always like myself for some things I say or do. But the Spirit quickens my soul and I quickly repent and ask forgiveness, and strength or wisdom to be an overcomer. It was a joy when I learned temptations had a purpose. We can help others because we have come through them and can truly give comfort. It allows God to strengthen our faith. To teach us that without him we are lost. And it makes us the better witness. Doesn't James 1:2 say, Count it all joy when ye fall into divers temptations. Verse 3: Knowing this, the trying of your faith worketh patience.

So we come full circle. The act of submission of our Lord Jesus Christ in accepting the cross. Experiencing the infliction of suffering, shedding his blood and death not only to gain a place in heaven for us, but to be our example. To encourage us. That we might be able to sing, Have thine own way, Lord. Thou art the Potter. I am the clay. Mold me and make me after thy will. While I am waiting yielded and still. Hallelujah!

With the wisdom born of true experience in the walk of faith, we find Leona's reminder to look to Jesus as our source, example, hope and comfort. In times of grief, she confirms that her faith holds fast, as she explains in the conclusion to the Sunday School discussion.

I looked again at those words in the hymn: *When* we walk with the Lord. In the light of his word. If there is a secret to living a victorious life, that is it. For we live in a world of sin, sickness, and brutality. Yet as a child of God we rely on the promises God has made. Sometimes they chasten us. Bring us under conviction that our ways are not his ways. Our thoughts are not his thoughts Isiah 55:8. It brings us back to his throne of grace and mercy. And we seek his forgiveness and find there the truth of his promise that if we come to him he will not cast us off John 6:37.

And I thought, walking in the light of his Word made all the difference in the world. How often it is his Word that stills our fears. The uncertainties of life. Gives comfort when nothing or no one can. We so often pray for our will. But peace comes when we surrender it to his will.

The other unspeakable joy came in the form of comfort when I learned that the driver of the van that hit my son's car when it spun out of control, knelt in the snow and prayed in my son's ear until the ambulance came to take him away. My daughter was there at the hospital before he died and she said, Mama, my brother had the most beautiful smile on his face and I knew he was safe in the arms of Jesus.

Oh precious is the flow, that makes me white as snow. No other Name I know. Nothing but the blood of Jesus. When life overwhelms I remember my Jesus kneeling in the Garden of Gethsemane. And being in agony he prayed more earnestly. And I am comforted. Jesus's love was so great he gave his life for us. May a resolve be born in all who call upon that precious name to surrender all to him that Jesus may truly be glorified on earth as he is in heaven.

Leona trusted God, dependent upon him and his sustaining power to live the Christian life. Reading her letters allows us a look into the chamber of her resolute faith, a faith lovingly poured upon her by the Savior. Once again it is the scriptures that safeguard and comfort her heart, and fuel her fervent desire for revival among all people.

One of the joys of reaching this age is to be able to look back and see how God has kept his promises, like Hebrews 13:5–6: …I will never leave thee nor forsake thee so that we may boldly say the Lord is my helper and I will not fear what man shall do unto me. One of my favorite Psalms is 91:1–4. One of God's names is El Shaddai meaning *all sufficient*. Those two words spell out a lifelong dependence on God.

Verse 1: He that dwelleth in the secret place of the Most High shall abide under the shadow of the Almighty. As a child, my mother would spread a blanket under the shade of a huge tree in our yard. She taught my sister and me to sew. We each had a celluloid doll with moveable arms and legs. We also had a cigar box to keep our materials and dolls in. We would set up for hours and fashion clothes out of the scraps of material while the huge tree sheltered us from the sun. How secure and happy we were.

Verse 2: I will say of the Lord, He is my refuge and my fortress. My God; in Him will I trust. When we think of protection it isn't just a place to flee to. But one where we feel safe and secure. What better or safer place can we be than in the arms of Jesus? His Word promised verse 3: Surely He shall deliver thee from the snare of the fowler and from the raging epidemics. Verse 4: He shall cover thee with His feathers, and under His wings shall thou trust; His truth shall be thy shield and buckler. Jesus once sat outside Jerusalem's gates and likened Himself to calling the lost children of Israel to Himself, as a hen gathers her chicks; but they would not Matthew 23:37.

Surely God weeps for our nation today. How earnestly we need to pray for a revival to sweep across not only our nation, but our world. May God hear our earnest prayers.

So we remember that Leona points us to the Lord whose gift of faith enables us to lay hold of the blessings and heavenly things here on earth. Let us receive joyously the wisdom imparted by one who leaves loving instructions to comfort and encourage us.

I have enjoyed being here in the mountains. It's exciting to see the finishing things being done to the new house. A house can never become a home until one lives in it. Experiences the good or rights the defects. But isn't that like faith. We experience the joy of being new creatures in Christ. At ten I really didn't know what they meant when I was told I was a sinner. I didn't steal, lie or do hurtful things, and in the innocence of children in those times all I really wanted to be sure of was that Jesus loved me. Easter took on a brand new meaning when I learned it wasn't a new dress, or an Easter bunny that set spring in motion. It was Jesus. Jesus who loved me and died for me so that I might one day live with him. It brought joy and peace and the realization I wanted very much to live for him. Hence it was with my faith. I learned to live and the Lord graciously led me through the defects (sins.) I marvel now at the temptations that could have been stumbling blocks had not my Lord been there to use them for building blocks in faith. Teaching me to lean on him. To run to him and not from him. To trust and obey. To pray my way through tough times. Psalm 111:10: The fear of the Lord is the beginning of wisdom; a good understanding have all they that do His commandments; His praise endureth forever. I claim this for my family too and praise God I believe He is more than able to do abundantly, above all that we ask or think, according to the power that worketh in us.

Reading the entire set of letters sent to Sally brings together a whole, marvelous tapestry of Leona's creative energies in writing, its own form of literature. I am swept into the power of her arguments, hunger for her counsel, become zealous for the vitality of Christian being and experience. Leona's unique hybrid method of commonplacing—some diary, some journal, a blended commonplace book—was her own way to collect wisdom learned from the Bible, life experience, books, other readings, or mentors who had advice to share. I begin to suspect that Leona's love for literature in school included journaling. After all, Mark Twain. Anne Frank, and Madeleine L'Engle is good company to keep. She might be surprised—and delighted—that her lifelong love for the written word became an unimaginable ministry. And perhaps, in a quiet, secret place, she hoped that someday her writing would survive as a legacy to inspire great-grandchildren and generations thereafter, who might raid her steamer-trunk of faith. And it surely refreshes and blesses those of us with eyes to see and ears to hear the Lord speaking through Grandma's letters.

I cannot remember a time that God has not been faithful. I wish I could say the same for me. But wonder of wonders his promise to keep me is still working today. He has taught us to be overcomers. He has walked in the valley of despair with us. He has given us mountain tops to glimpse the wonders of his love. He sent angels to strengthen Christ in his moments of despair. Looking back, I *know* he has provided many times "angels" people to touch my life. Experiences to help me grow in faith. Faith that draws me closer to him. Faith that gives a peace that passeth all understanding, in the middle of darkness. Or strength to forbear when it is most needed. As my oldest granddaughter says, "What are you trying to teach me now?" Instead of, "Why me?" One thing I know for sure. I'll not graduate from the Lord's schoolroom of life until I land feet first or bottom up in the place he has prepared for those who love him. It is something that fills my heart and spills out first thing in the morning and the last thing at night. Lord I love you and thank you for Jesus. May each day draw us closer to him.

Sincerely in his Name,
Leona Moats

CHAPTER 7

The Joybells

From start to finish, Leona took great care in crafting her essays. Opening paragraphs capture our attention with a universal appeal to the events, joys, and challenges of everyday family life. The heart of the composition instructs us through the scripture, hymns, and songs she chooses and applies to the Christian walk of faith in all provinces of a believer's life. She often concludes in a manner intended to lay the hands of benediction upon the reader, with whom she cherishes the beautiful bonds of devotion with Christ's people everywhere.

Hallelujah! What a Savior we have! No empty promises. May this ring the joybells in your heart.

Oh hallelujah! We have the comfort and reassurance Jesus is mine and I am his. May that lift your soul and ring the joybells in your spirit.

Oh how I love Jesus *because* he *first loved me*. May that ring the joybells in your heart as we look to the time when we shall see Jesus, and sing saved by grace.

With our future secure in Jesus, we are blessed with a peace only he can give. Doesn't that cause the joybells to ring in your heart?

So we celebrate again the gift of God to all who will receive him and continue to share that with a world that needs to know the love of God in Christ. May that set the joybells ringing in your heart and spirit.

Set the joybells ringing in your heart. It's an unusual affectation, a unique phrase I'd never heard before. So it set the "investigation bells" a pealing in my own heart, and I traverse the venerable pathways in the hymnody of the church.

Nearly every letter I receive from Leona and just about every letter I read in the big white notebook contains at least one reference to a hymn or spiritual song. Leona loved the music of worship in the church. She couldn't read music, but she loved the words and followed the melodies by ear. Over time, she memorized the great and transcendent songs of faith. Understanding innately the power of music to shape the affections of the human heart, she carefully taught both Scripture and spiritual songs to her children. The letters lay before us the witness to the power of hymns to reinforce scriptural truths and strengthen the believer's life. It is a part of worshiping God "in the beauty of holiness" (Psalm 96:9).

Perhaps we neglect to appreciate the full realm of God's attributes, and one of those overlooked facets is God's delight in all things beautiful. God loves beauty and tells us so in the descriptions of the Old Testament structures and furnishings of the tabernacle. He endowed skilled artisans with the abilities to craft these works. The priests who served in the tabernacle and later the temple dressed not in everyday clothes but in garments made "for glory and beauty" (Exodus 28:2). The art forms of color and design skillfully wrought are clearly pleasing to God. The Lord who created us also knows the essence and power of music within our spirit to "make melody in our hearts to the Lord" (Ephesians 5:19). Music is an element of the beauty of the Lord.

But while construction and the crafting of objects proceeds from the craftsman's hand, God designed the beauty of music to proceed from within the spirit of man, a welling up of praise from the marrow of the heart. There are heartfelt songs composed by Moses, Miriam, and Deborah recorded in Scripture. The appointment of a young talented court musician in 1 Samuel 16, David, wrote psalms that are the anchor for our worship today. David composed psalms used in the public worship of God with particular instruments to be used and specific vocal accompaniment in mind. He dedicated the arts of his poetry and music to the worship of the Lord. The New Testament songs of Zechariah, Mary, and Simeon are forever hallowed in Scripture; and though there is no musical notation, we can feel the magnificent emotion welling up from each of these composers. Songs of praise, songs of thanksgiving, songs of faith—as well as songs of despair, lament, and contrition—all speak from that section in the human spirit filled only by music.

Enter Martin Luther and the Reformation. Martin Luther loved music and was a reformer of musical practice in the church. He played instruments, sang, and composed music, including hymns. He went so far as to assert that music was "the living voice of the Gospel." The great purpose of text and musical accompaniment was simply to praise God and proclaim his Word. Luther decried the Roman church music chanted by monks in Latin and mostly useless to the common worshiper. He stood firm on the simple premise that both music and the lyrics should be plain and down-to-earth in style, understandable by that common worshiper, and Luther was ostensibly the first to assert an understanding of the powerful effect of music on youth. He insisted that the music of the church was of great benefit to youth, ridding their minds of unholy, sensuous songs, and drawing them to acquaintance with the good and joyous music that praises God its Maker.

Luther collaborated with several acclaimed composers of the time, among them Johann Walter, Conrad Rupsch, and Justus Jonas. Writing what he called "chorales" (and what we would later call hymns), chorales were to be sung by the congregation. These songs were simple, singable melodies with plainly understandable text. The singing was assisted by choirs—except that the choirs were *within* the congregation in order to provide training and support for the worshipers, all of it *a cappella.* Imagine the power of "A Mighty Fortress Is Our God" in this worship setting. Though he played musical instruments, Luther stuck to singing in church without instrumental aid. He lived his love of music, believing that it was a powerful shaper of hearts and minds in worship.

John Calvin joined Luther in the reformation of church music and worship. He also acknowledged the power of music to inspire worshiper's hearts in praise to God's glory. Singing and songs should cause the worshiper to meditate on God's works and bring us to love, fear, and honor him. Few would disagree with Calvin on this score. Calvin favored singing Psalms but did move later to an acceptance of hymns and spiritual songs. Calvin's (like Luther's) great concern was that the songs themselves should be simple and easy to sing, with meaning understood by the common parishioner. Music was to be used with a clear apprehension of the majesty of God, with a respectfulness befitting the place and act of worship. Like Luther, Calvin also believed children were to benefit from the music and singing, powerful tools for instruction in God's truth. Luther and Calvin certainly understood the training up of youth.

Others followed the reformers' lead. Isaac Watts, whose work spanned the period from the late seventeenth century into the mid eighteenth century, is renowned as the "Father of English Hymnody." He wrote more than six hundred hymns at a time in English history when the Dissenters roiled the waters in opposition to the Anglican Church of England. Raised in a Dissenter home, he remained an independent for the rest of his life, becoming senior pastor at Mark Lane Independent Chapel in London.

Watts became "troubled" by the congregational singing in the church. By the early 1700s, the Lutheran churches had been singing hymns for more than a hundred years, but Watts was distressed by the Calvinist tradition in nonconformist churches of singing only the Psalms. After being handed a challenge by his father (also a minister) to do something about it, Watts embarked upon what became a two-year project to write a new hymn for each Sunday worship service. He published these (at the timely age of twenty-three) from 1707–1709. For Watts, it was all about singing the whole experience of worship, which should "elevate us to the most delightful and divine sensations." Hymns brought a personal religious experience to worship. This departure from the safety of singing the Psalms stirred controversy well beyond the end of Watts's life, a disputation which still exists among Protestant denominations today. And like Luther and Calvin, Watts believed that children ought to be included in singing praise to God, schooled early to "devotion that kindles piety." He published *Divine and Moral Songs for Children* in 1715. It sold eighty thousand copies in the first year. It is still available for purchase. Hymns such as "O God Our Help in Ages Past," "Joy to the World," "When I Survey the Wondrous Cross," "O Bless the Lord My Soul," and "Am I a Soldier of the Cross" still unite worshipers in praise and adoration, a legacy of Watts's prolific hymn-writing pen.

Then came the Methodists. John Wesley is well known and the recognizable visage of Methodism, but his brother Charles Wesley, born in 1707, the eighteenth of nineteen children, may have been the invigorating force within the sphere of the brothers' religious awakenings. Their father was an Anglican clergyman. Charles was schooled at home by his mother, primarily in the classical languages, and entered Christ College, Oxford, in the late 1720s. It was there that Charles formed a prayer group which became known somewhat acerbically as the "Holy Club" or "Methodists" for the member's regular and devoted practice of religious activities. Charles's brother, John, and George Whitefield were prominent members of the group.

Ordained a priest in the Church of England in 1735, it was not until May 1738 that Charles claimed a true conversion experience. He wrote his first hymn to celebrate the event. What followed was nearly nine thousand more hymns over a fifty-year period. Methodists loved hymnody, becoming known for their exuberance in singing Wesley's hymns. So did other churches. Wesley's hymns are grounded in the fundaments of the Christian faith, and they speak to the emotion and personal experience of the common worshiper. Like Luther's, Wesley's hymns expressed plain ideas the singer could grasp and own in faith. It was said that the power of Charles's hymns taught the people as much as John's preaching and writings.

Among his much-loved hymns are "Come, Thou Long Expected Jesus," "O for a Thousand Tongues to Sing," "Jesus, Lover of My Soul," "Christ the Lord Is Risen Today," and "Hark! The Herald Angels

Sing." If Isaac Watts is honored as the Father of English Hymnody, Wesley earns the title "the Asaph of the Methodist Church" and the appellation Greatest Hymn Writer of All Time.

Over the last three hundred years, what Luther started has flourished. Hundreds of authors—men and women—have composed hymns and music, now a cherished part of worship in the Christian church. The enlargement of hymnody included the writers William Cowper ("There Is a Fountain"), Augustus Toplady ("Rock of Ages"), Fanny Crosby ("Blessed Assurance"), Frances Havergal ("Take My Life and Let It Be"). John Wesley contributed "O Lord Within Thy Sacred Gates." J. Wilbur Chapman wrote the words to the much-loved hymn "Jesus! What a Friend for Sinners!" Chapman was a little-known Presbyterian minister and evangelist in the late 1800s and early 1900s. He preached in D. L. Moody's crusades where he witnessed the power of music and subsequently spread this influence in collaboration with the work of fellow evangelist Billy Sunday. Charles Spurgeon's pen paused from his prolific preaching and writing missions to compose *Our Own Hymnbook*—for the Metropolitan Tabernacle—and his composition, the much-loved "Amidst Us Our Beloved Stands," still stirs hearts. This book too is still in print today.

The controversy over music in the church began in Martin Luther's time and remains throughout the confessing Protestant church. Psalter only or hymns too? *A cappella* or with instrumentation? Nearly all agree, however, that singing together in worship as part of the family of God instructs our hearts with the truths of the words sung. Hymns, songs, and spiritual songs become a treasured source of spiritual nurture. Through them we are bound together in times of hardship, bearing one another's burdens as well as in times of joy. Leona speaks to the power of music to infuse a deep appreciation of grace.

> At our Sunday evening service, we were asked to choose a hymn and tell why it was important to us. There are countless ones that speak so wonderfully of the love I found in Jesus; the one I chose was "Saved by Grace." That

wonderful grace drew me in as a child, kept me through my troubled teenage years, taught me, led me, chastised me, renewed my spirit day by day over the trying times of life, gave me hope life could still be beautiful when a loved one was taken away—a mother, grandparent, son. This morning I was praying for a grandchild's family and for the little ones. The list grows sweeter as the days go by, for now it includes great-grandchildren. I do so want them to have a faith in Jesus, not just a religion. Then the Lord caused me to remember times both in my own life, the children's, the grandchildren's, and a wonderful peace flowed into my heart. I wept, remembering the promises the Lord has made and kept. The Bible says in Hebrews 13:8, "Jesus Christ is the same yesterday, today, and forever." That same wonderful grace that has never failed will not fail now. When I chose that hymn, I said I never want to forget it was God's grace that sought me, kept me, and bought me. Nothing I did, can do, or will do could merit that kind of love from my Father in heaven.

Fanny Crosby wrote the words to "Saved by Grace." The music was composed by George C. Stebbins, a contemporary of, among others, Ira D. Sankey.

In 1899, J. Edward Ruark wrote the words to "You May Have the Joy Bells," the beloved song which seems rooted in Leona's collection of hymns. William J. Kirkpatrick composed the music, a music collaborator for several hymn writers of the time. With words secured in the Scriptures, Leona made melody in her heart to the Lord. Singing psalms, prayers, and hymns reflects God's love of beauty back to him with grateful hearts.

Leona loved hymns; so do I. It was "hymns and spiritual songs" that backed me unawares into the power of the Gospel toward salvation.

Few photographs survive from the time of my mother's youth, but those that do invariably include her beloved dog Scrappy and her guitar. Some things manage to cut across socioeconomic borders, and despite living in poverty in the western Alleghenies, my mother possessed a nice-looking six-string guitar. Her 1940 South Fayette Township High School senior yearbook records the inscription: "Julia Matesia wills her love for music to anyone who is interested." She was likely self-taught since the high school sponsored only a separate boy's and girl's chorus and a fifteen-member orchestra. I remember her ability to play an old pump-pedal organ, a melodium, a dilapidated relic unwanted by the owner of her rooming house in Detroit. After she married, it made the trip to the home my parents built in 1953 in Troy.

The newly consolidated Troy Township schools benefited from the suburban building boom north of Detroit farmland that was turned into platted subdivisions. Schools were renovated and programs enlarged, befitting post-WWII expansion and a prospering economy. One afternoon, home from fourth grade, I handed over to my mother a notice about an evening meeting at the school for parents and students interested in the band program. I don't remember an overwhelming attraction to anything musical, but we came home that evening with a clarinet for me, the case shiny brown leather-look plastic. I took it into the bedroom, opened it, fingered all five parts mouthpiece to bell, touched with awe the tangle of silver keys. I put each piece back perfectly in the felt-lined cradles. I am deaf to the muffled angry voices in the kitchen. The cost of the clarinet came to five dollars a month, two years to pay off the $127 cost. The agreement allowed free return of the instrument within three months if the student quit the program.

It's an old maxim that some forms of art or the aptitude toward them pass from one generation to the next. That may or may not be so, but I must believe that somewhere my mother's musical dower grafted in me. Once past beginning band, my musical career moved swiftly through concert band, to symphony band, to first-chair concert mistress as a high school senior. During summer band camps, we were allowed to borrow school-owned instruments to try out for fun. I taught myself to play the oboe, bassoon, and French horn, lured by their mellow, honeyed voices. High School freshman year, the marching band lacks members in the brass section. I pick up my sister's cornet with the dented bell (the result of a car accident—a new silver trumpet comes of that) and march that season third cornet. But after class one winter January day in my senior year, band director Larry L. Dickerson calls me aside to inform me that he is nominating me for the United States Collegiate Wind Band, a program sponsored by Purdue University and composed of collegiate and high school musicians from across the country. The band's itinerary for three weeks in August 1971 is a concert performance tour of five European and Russian capitals: London, Brussels, Paris, Amsterdam, and Moscow. I am accepted for membership. The cost of the three-week tour is a thousand dollars. Bake sales are held. Local businesses buy my airline tickets. The "hat is passed" in the teacher's lounge at Troy High School several times. I make the trip, a wide-eyed and homesick concert performer, one dress and two pairs of walking shoes in my suitcase, half a world away with music.

I return home in late August just in time for the start of freshman year at Central Michigan University in Mount Pleasant, Michigan. I return my clarinet to its case, never to pick it up again. But I enjoy music, being able to read music, appreciating the vast and literate world of music and the beauty it contributes to the lives of people everywhere. I love the special corpus of religious and sacred music written to inspire worship and praise to the Lord. Going back fifty years, it is band and music that conspired together in the most precious of lifetime experiences.

One February Sunday evening, a friend in band class invited me to the evening worship service at her church. She and other members of our high school band are to play at the revival-style service, and a woodwind is needed. There are more evening performances throughout the week. I walk the snow-covered mile-and-a-half down a busy main road to the church and back home afterward, clutching my clarinet in its frozen brown plastic case. My mother, working nights, couldn't object to my attendance at a Baptist church. It was, after all, a musical performance. At the end of the week, I walk forward, approach the Anxious Bench, and bow my head, the signal I wish to receive Christ as my Savior. Afterward, my friend Nancy's mother pats me on the back. Music was instrumental in the saving of my soul.

Leona may not have been able to read music, but she could follow the lead of instrumental accompaniment, reading the text of the great hymns of old in the hymn book. Over time, she memorized the hymns and music that spoke so deeply to her heart. Even Augustine, who considered banning music from worship, relented when he came to the conclusion:

> When religious texts are sung well, greater religious devotion is inspired. Souls are moved, and with a warmer devotion kindled to piety than if they are not so sung.

I wish I could once again stand next to Leona and together sing words and music to lift our hearts in worship and praise to the Lord. We have each gotten to this place though by very different paths. The words from my church's concluding hymn last Lord's Day, sung in parts and with piano accompaniment, would have pleased Leona and, most of all, our Lord.

Jesus! What a Friend for Sinners!

Jesus! What a Friend for sinners! Jesus! Lover of
    my soul;
Friends may fail me, foes assail me, he, my Savior,
    makes me whole.

Hal—le—lu—jah! What a Savior! Hal—le—
    lu—jah! what a Friend!
Saving, helping, keeping, loving, he is with me
    to the end.
Jesus! I do now receive him, more than all in him
    I find;
he hath granted me forgiveness, I am his, and he
    is mine.
Hal—le—lu—jah! What a Savior! Hal—le—
    lu—jah! what a Friend!
Saving, helping, keeping, loving, he is with me
    to the end.

CHAPTER 8

Grandma's Best Quotes and Notes

I approach the reading of God's Word this morning with a longing for the outpouring of grace. Time and life experience have made sweet the communion with God's Word. This has not always been so. I am long past the newness of this portion of the Christian walk that begins as we learn to know ourselves as first God knows us. With our eyes opened by his grace, then we know the Creator and his love for us through Christ. In God's wisdom, this is a progressive unveiling tempered by the rigors of everyday life. We are not the first to trek along this path. That great cloud of witnesses recorded in Hebrews appears—Abraham, Moses, David, and ultimately, the Lord Jesus—all journeys of faith, all examples to strengthen and encourage our hearts, all a record of that which is common to man: lessons; hardships; joys and celebrations; doubts, fears, worries, uncertainties; times of testing; obstacles to overcome. With overcoming and endurance emerges the blessings. It is a gradual sense that we are called to follow the Lord where he leads us.

Through this journey, we experience—not just observe—God's fatherly care for us, his furnishing, accord, and even reclamation of us. It is an awareness that grows over time—that this world is not our own, and we prepare for a far better one to come even while we live and serve him in this one here, now, today. So we are not without a goal; there is clearly a destination and, with that, a sense of security and rest and even peace.

This is the great work of the Christian life, the participation in it filled with spiritual exuberance. It is fostered by a deep commitment to the Scriptures that summon us to pursue godliness and holiness without which no one will see God (Hebrews 12:14). This is what I see in Leona's lifelong walk of faith. She left a gracious roadmap of a life in service and fidelity to God.

There is an old-fashioned phrase associated with this life of surrender—piety. Perhaps it has fallen out of favor, replaced by more "modern" terms like spirituality or zeal or devotion, but these words are not the same as piety. True piety is more than devout fulfillment of religious duties. Its impulses rise from a reverence and love for God, a deep and heartfelt affection. It is expressed in joy and sincerity in living out our faith and is framed by the Scriptures, the sacraments, and prayer. The result is the fruit of the Spirit in our lives.

A warm and personal piety comes from reverence for Scripture, and it is Scripture that teaches us the irreproachable disposition of our holy God. It commands us to be holy as he is holy, and by the Holy Spirit, we are given the means to grow in this holiness. Piety is expressed in grateful obedience, serving with a loving heart, doing good works in gratitude for his goodness toward us in Christ. Christians are drawn to piety because we see it in Jesus's life and desire it because it emulates and honors him. True piety is an outworking of humility that gives its authentic presence its beauty. If piety is the walk of the Christian life, its sandals are the Christian virtues which conform our lives to Christ. Leona pursued piety; it is this which drew me to her life's example. She loved the Lord by endeavoring to keep his commandments and, thereby, confirmed that piety is more than being very religious or deeply devout. An oft-quoted summary of the Christian life by John Calvin addresses it directly: "I offer thee my heart, Lord, promptly and sincerely." This is the essence of piety that moved Leona and, ultimately, moves all believers.

On the tract table in the foyer at my friend Nancy's church, the little Baptist church where I met the Lord, a collection of printed materials was an oasis to me. I remember a great thirst for the spiritual drink which now claimed my heart and interest. Settled in neat stacks on the table was a selection of booklets and tracts, the most attractive of which was a monthly publication titled *Our Daily Bread*. There was nothing in my home to feed my spiritual hunger. The Catholic Missal in my mother's bookcase was written partly in English, partly in Latin, arranged in a perplexing and difficult order. But the *Our Daily Bread* booklets were small enough to slip into a purse as a discreet companion to accompany me anywhere. This ingenious collection of Scripture studies was a lifeline. I was introduced to Scripture, to prayer, to the fundamentals of Christian belief; and it sustained me until away at my freshman year in college, I acquired my first Bible.

Leona too found edification, comfort, and ideas from the studies in *Our Daily Bread*; and from time to time in her letters, the magazine *Guideposts* also afforded a topic or idea which she incorporated in her writings. Leona's letters bear a resemblance to these study guides and were possibly an inspiration for her own literary efforts.

Her letters declare a constant and deep concern for the Gospel and its impact on culture and society. She lived through a lifetime of momentous historical changes and worked out the interpretation of those events in relation to what she considered the "center of the universe"—the Christian faith and her family. The letters give us a living history not to be found in any other place or source, satisfying a deep and enduring human need for roots. She had a manner of gathering thoughts together, forging word pictures and sensory experiences for the reader. She is pithy, earthy, and full of the emotion of true piety. Leona may have admired authors and other publications, but her work stands in its own dignified and unique place.

The great strength of Leona's body of work is the pattern of living laid out in the pages week by week. The installments gave me time between them to think about my own life in relation to the exercise of faithful living. She eases into writing about the familiar issues of family life then moves to matters on her heart affecting the good and well-being of her audience—suffering, temptation, trials, comfort, hope, and the sufficiency of faith in Christ; a recognition of the Christian biblical pattern that suffering leads to obedience and obedience to hope; trials lead to tempering and tempering to submission, endurance, and wisdom. It is the sagacity shared by an elder in the faith.

> When someone says "have a good day," whether it is a neighbor, clerk, or friend, I always say thank you. I'm bound to. The Lord made it.
>
> I would rather be as clay in the hands of God than stand on my own with the wealth of the world.
>
> God is faithful in the small things as well as the big issues that come our way.
>
> Does his answer to prayer always fit our plan? No, but sooner or later we learn to say, "Not my will but Thine be done."
>
> I think sometimes the Lord allows our lives to go through a type of spring cleaning to help us sort through what we deem important in the light of his grace. The end result brings our priorities back into focus, and we find ourselves asking, "Lord, make me a better steward of all that I am in talent, time, and material things."

At times her laconic insights carry a gentle rebuke.

> It's easier to get people to go to a game than to come to church.
>
> My grandmother's advice: don't get so heavenly minded you're no earthly good. I'm thankful it set my course in life.

The natural world held a special place for Leona. She cultivated a reverent sense of the Creator and his workmanship, a witness to his power and rule over the earth. God's presence in his world inspired in her a sense of safety and security in his abiding care.

> Think of each day as a special gift from God and unwrap it gratefully.

I woke up to a sunrise and watched the day-break, bright and beautiful. A lovely old hymn filled the recesses of my mind:

When morning gilds the skies, my soul awakes and cries, may Jesus Christ be praised.

Having lived a quarter of a century in the country, driving to work in the morning offered a fresh look on the day. Seeing the sun break across the eastern horizon, smelling the freshness of the air, watching the mist rise off the fields, hearing the meadowlark's sweet song. What an awesome God we have. He created so much beauty to enjoy.

When I think of protection, it isn't just a place to flee to but one where we feel safe and secure. What better or safer place can we be than in the arms of Jesus?

He shall cover thee with His feathers, and under His wings shall thou trust; his truth shall be thy shield and buckler. (Psalm 91:4)

The earth is the Lord's and the fullness thereof, the world and they that dwell therein. (Psalm 24:1)

That is *us*—you and me. Doesn't that over-whelm you to remember it is God who creates, gives life, wisdom, and strength? It is he who holds it altogether and sustains his creation in us?

After retirement, Leona and her husband indulged in the delight of travel, particularly camping. The reader is swept up in the awe and reverence she felt for the sheer beauty and expression of nature that she discovered along these journeys.

> Sitting in the quiet of my living room, memories floated in and out of my thoughts— the times spent in summer and fall in northern forests, the wildflowers along the paths, the pungent smell of pine, the clear blue lakes, the sight of birds, the sound of loons at dusk. Tiny flowers cover the ground like a floral carpet out of my grandmother's time. We stood at the foot of the glacier fields in Washington, drove through the redwood forest, walked the sandy beaches of California and felt the tide on our bare feet, smelled the sweetness of the citrus orchards in full bloom, marveled at how a little rain could make the desert bloom. It has taken years of travel to cover all this ground, yet the God we know spoke *a word* and called it all into being. I marveled at the Lord who created all this as the same One who holds the world in his hands today. Why would such a God who had such power send his Son to be rejected, beaten, condemned, forsaken, even crucified in the cruelest manner? Why? Because a price had to be paid that we might be redeemed to become his family—not because he needs us *but because* he *wants* us. Can you fathom a love like that?

I am asked what I find so compelling in a collection of handwritten letters produced by a woman in the middle of the last century, a woman from the rural heartland of America with an eleventh-grade education, growing up with less-than-modest means. Leona made her way through this life, leaving a priceless record of the lessons of the Christian experience. She faced challenges and hardships and developed a store of inner strength. She made an interesting, fulfilling life through effort, sacrifice, and hard work. It is her description of the Refiner's fire of tribulation and suffering where the precious gems of experience shine best.

> Heartbreak and disappointments take their toll, but God uses them to shape us into vessels he can use.
>
> There have been times in all our lives when we felt the ground of faith literally being washed out from under us, yet our Anchor held.

> Count your blessings name them one by one...see what God has done... Count your blessings...and you'll be surprised to see what God has done.

> My grandma didn't just sing those songs. She acted on them and advised me to do that when life became difficult. She taught me another great truth—don't do things expecting gratitude; do it for Christ's sake. The one you help may never thank you. If you do it for the wrong reasons, you'll miss the joy of doing. Somewhere down the line it will come back to you. If there is a real fault in our faith walk, it may be because society gives us a quick fix like instant oatmeal or microwave dinners. I've had prayers answered while I was still on my knees, but others were slow in coming. In the latter, we learn the wonderful truth of 2 Corinthians 5:7—we walk by faith, not by sight.
>
> (In Sunday school) we are asked to think what Jesus did for us. I've a lifetime of experiences to draw from. We ask, why are we allowed to suffer? Hebrews 5:8:

> Though he were a son, yet He learned obedience by the things He suffered.

> When you think of what that obedience cost Jesus, who are we to question why God allows us to go through trials—yes, and even suffer? But Jesus looked beyond the suffering and saw the glory before him. Jesus paid for all our sins. I don't always like myself for some things I say or do, but the Spirit quickens my soul, and I quickly repent and ask forgiveness *and* strength or wisdom to be an overcomer. It was a joy when I learned that temptations had a purpose. The trying of your faith worketh patience.

Leona created handwritten original drafts which she photocopied to send on to those on her mailing list. Before folding and inserting each letter into its envelope, she almost always added a handwritten personal note as a postscript. These notes are among my most cherished portions of her writings.

> My time (here in Michigan) is running out. A week from today, I will be going to Omaha to another granddaughter's and looking forward to her dogs and parrots. My life is so full, and I count you a special part of that. May the Lord bless you and keep you in his wonderful care.

A gracious personal thought after returning to Omaha:

> I am so thankful to have had a bit of time with you and to be able to praise God together. It is a joy to see you again. You are a blessing.

A postscript almost as long as the letter itself:

> The Lord willing and if Heidi & Jeff are
> able to come, I will go to Michigan with them
> for a while. I look forward not only to be with
> them, but seeing friends I have made there.
> What a life!! No complaints. Heartaches yes.
> Disappointments. But God has been with me
> all the way, and promised I shall see Jesus and
> tell the story "saved by grace." Wow!! How good
> it was to hear from you. Remember God is as
> close as the prayer in your heart. And I'm not
> sure but you need the prayer more than these
> students who are testing your patience. One day
> I am sure they will count themselves blessed to
> have had you for a teacher. Hang in there honey.
> Hold tight to the windows God gives you in your
> art and remember Jesus brought you this far. He
> won't leave you now.

The letters originally intended to keep in touch with friends and family, but those of us who received her dispatches recognized the universal and timeless vitality of the writings. Many of us began to collect the letters. Some of us still cling to them as to a lifeline. More than a connection to the past, they are a spur to reach for the future our faith holds for us. That is Leona's great endowment to us.

Leona wrote to comfort and extend a sense of Christ's love to others and to confirm and proclaim the power of the Gospel, to affirm the power of God to bless us and keep us all the days of our journey in this life. She wrote to fulfill the urgency that all writers feel to connect with their readers through the grace of the written word.

> These is something about age. It can make
> our future brighter despite health or problems,
> physical or spiritual. I prefer to set my sights
> on the promises of Jesus and trust him for the

strength for today, the patience to run the course, holding the promises of the future close to my heart.

That is the testimony of my life. Through great joy, much love in friends and family, my God has been a constant source of help and encouragement. When life brought tragedy, *he* was there. When temptation beset me, Jesus was there. When my cup runneth over, it was the love of Jesus. He has *never* failed. We know the truth of my little great-grandson's words: God is good—all the time.

Legacy is not a matter of what is left *for* others; it is a matter of what we leave *in* others.

CHAPTER 9

The Journey: One More Conversation

Leona's life journey on this earth, by God's grace, was a sojourn of more than ninety-five years. She lived a great deal of it—most of it, in fact, before we met at the Friday night evening prayer fellowship. It was no mere coincidence that we met but a great and generous providence. I am brought into her life's passage through church and through her family. I learned that Leona saw the challenges of life as part of the progress to a greater goal—the testing and refining of our hearts in preparation for glory and eternal joy in the presence of God. Her writings travel the gentle camber of grace from one headland to the other side, over and above the turbulent rivers of life.

The Reverend Jeffrey B. Wilson, Leona's grandson-in-law, began a sermon to our congregation recently by musing:

> Did you know what was ahead of you at the beginning of your Christian life? Temptations, struggles; confrontations with evil and injustice. Severe doubts, spiritual malaise, scintillating allurements that would entice you, fears and discouragements. The day you will die. Did you know these things before you began your Christian journey?

He goes on:

> No matter how old you were when you were baptized, you did not know what was ahead. Wouldn't it be nice if someone could give you a topographical map of the journey, with all the contours showing the trail, where the cliffs and rivers are, the poisonous plants and wild animals, the troublemakers encamped. The problems you will face and the date they will show up. Christians through the ages have understood their Christian life as a journey. Our life with the Lord is a journey, step-by-step from beginning to end.

A journey is a passage, a travel from one place in time to another. No one escapes this passage; no Christian eludes the appointed progression. Almost all the historic fathers of the faith relate their own personal experiences as that of an odyssey in this life in which God works to draw the pilgrim to himself. There is a measure of great comfort and assurance in God's Word in Hebrews 12:1–2:

> Therefore we also, since we are surrounded by so great a cloud of witnesses, let us lay aside every weight, and the sin which so easily ensnares us, and let us run with endurance the race that is set before us, looking unto Jesus, the author and finisher of our faith, who for the joy that was set before Him endured the cross, despising the shame, and has sat down at the right hand of the throne of God. (NKJV)

A "great cloud of witnesses" who point us to Christ, who instruct us to run with endurance, reject sin, and pursue godly living in grateful obedience to Christ for all that he has accomplished for us. Our Christian walk unfolds before us, an everlasting path. God creates in us a thirst for his righteousness, a love for him, for his people, and for the world in need of a Savior. It is a deliberate and conscious effort enabled by God's grace. He supplies the desire, means, and strength to take on this task of obedience. Among the means are the dear saints treading the same trail alongside us.

Leona became one of those witnesses to me. Her letters became like a road map for living, she herself a mentor in the faith, whose example of walking with Jesus helped satisfy a thirst for the fellowship I ached for. The letters develop into a conversation, the sound of a resonant voice, a weekly installment of inspiration in the grit and stamina of faith. Oh, how those of us who received the letters over the years would cherish one more conversation once again to soak up the poise, discernment, and authority of her words.

There are stories about family things I never experienced, the likes of which were a loving community unknown in my own family existence. Leona was a woman of dignity, humility, and wry humor. She was the mother figure I longed for. Best of all, what shone through was faith and love for Jesus, so true and pure, a place of rest in the midst of the weariness of life. I became convinced there are many others like me who would be refreshed by these waters, a union of storytelling and biblical truth.

Leona loved literature. The inspiration of literature is the great catalyst for all writers. Great literature mirrors the classical toil through the vicissitudes of life, the very same matters with which we all wrestle in our prosaic lives. In her writings, Leona didn't hold back. She spoke plainly and candidly. She handled difficult topics with evenness, compassion, and empathy. In the desire for one last conversation, I hear the providential presence of her voice. The letters are rich lode of persuasion and renewal, a simple buoyant imprint of an everyday matriarch.

The unique and distinguishing mark of the letters is the devout simplicity of the narrative. The familiar daily trials come to us through the gentleness of the stories beneath which lie profound lessons of living faith. We hear Leona's esteem for those who left such an example to light her own pathway.

> I count my blessings and remember my beloved grandma sharing this wisdom with me when my children were small. She said, "Honey, when things get difficult, remember to count your blessings, and you will find you have more to be thankful for than sorry about." This from a woman whose husband was killed on duty as a town marshal. It left her a widow with a two-and-a-half-year-old and five other children to raise. No pension, insurance, or assistance. She worked very hard to raise her family and to put the two younger through college before the Depression left her poverty-stricken. Even then, she would take what little she had and make wonderful cake doughnuts. She would go down the street and sell them, buy more flour, or whatever she needed, and make more doughnuts. Even in those hard times, she would scrape together enough to help a neighbor. Maybe it was sickness or a death— she would reach out to them. Through it all, her strong faith held. The lessons she taught sustained me. One day I am going to see the pearly gates she taught me about and walk the streets of gold with her.

A long life will give evidence of the intersections, detours, and crossroads of the voyage. Leona had her share. With characteristic aplomb and dignity, she reports on difficult times and the sustaining assurance of Christ's sufficiency to see her through.

> It started out with a light rain. I usually don't like those kinds of days. Years ago, I had a nervous breakdown on a day like that. I called my husband

at work. He came home and found me exhausted from working all night, trying to do the washing, ironing, and cleaning, unable to talk. All I could remember was to call Ronald. It was a long road back. I learned to talk without stuttering, be able to go places alone, to ride on the streetcar. Mercy, what a long time ago that was. It's been seventy-eight years since I took Jesus for my Savior. I can honestly say the verse in Hebrews 13:5 best describes a promise never broken:

Let your conversation be without covetousness and be content…for He hath said I will never leave thee nor forsake thee. So that we may boldly say, the Lord is my helper, and I will not fear what man shall do to me.

Hallelujah! What a wonderful message we received! What a wonderful gift to give—not just to our own but also a weary world that needs the light of Christ to lead them to the throne of God. May this set the joybells ringing in your heart, knowing the joy of the future is greater than any we have known here.

It takes a lifetime of learning and living to understand deeply that God cares for and preserves us on our pilgrimage in the faith. The life "vignettes" within the letters teach us that God cares what happens to his people and that he governs all things to bring about his purposes. More than thirty years of letters covers a lot of territory. Reflection is inevitable and quite useful in writing about the reality of God's keeping grace.

I'm sorry to admit it, but I am becoming a slow mover. How did that happen? But we can all be thankful God has a plan and a purpose for this time in life. We can choose to waste it on a pity party or joyfully accept our limitations and use them to God's glory through prayer and reaching out in love to those who need to know God loves them where they are and will help them to be what he wants them to be.

Once I looked back and was able to share with a young teenager that my life was very similar to hers. I wasn't raised in a Christian home. My father was an alcoholic; my mother ran a bar. I loved my mother very much, and she set good values in my life. Yet God kept me through those years. I even learned to remember how much I once loved my father, and God healed the bitterness in my spirit toward my father. He would do the same for her. Wonder of wonders, after all that time, I could see God had a purpose for allowing it in my life, and I could honestly thank the Lord for preparing me for such a time as this.

And in another vignette:

It's Sunday evening. There is light in our lives today—Sandy is home! Bill and I had a working partnership: he cooked, and I did the dishes. He only served a Depression dinner once—beef stew over rice, green beans, and leftover dessert from the Fourth of July. It brought to mind one evening in late fall in my childhood. Mother kept my sister and I at her restaurant. When she had a paying customer, she sent me across the street to buy a block of pressed coal to keep the restaurant's potbelly stove going. The only thing she had to give us was a half pint of whipping cream. She whipped it and let us eat the whole thing! Wow, did we feel special! She saved the hamburger for paying customers. We never felt deprived. I don't think that word was in a working family's vocabulary of that day.

Just the thought (of these times) takes me back to when Jesus came into the heart of a ten-year-old girl, the unspeakable joy that welled up in me. I had no idea how his presence in my heart and life would sustain me in the years that lay ahead. The journey of life cannot be experienced fully without life's pitfalls, mountaintop experiences, heart-wrenching trials, where we would *never* have found a way *without the Savior* who carried us through. The hard experiences were not to destroy us but to shape *us* and make *us*—*yes, you* and *myself*—into a *vessel only God can use to draw others in.*

As believers, our daily walk with the Lord includes the inevitable times of sufferings, troubles, and disappointments. We know to pray but sometimes pause in doubt and frustration, even questioning God's wisdom. At times we anguish when results don't go the way we think they should. How easily and quickly we forget the character of God before whom we present our petitions! More than once Grandma reminds us about the perspective we are to adopt toward disappointment because both she and Jesus have walked that path before us. No "pity party!" Receive the comfort of God's word. Humbly accept God's will because it is for his glory and our good. Let the trials through which you pass be a training ground, and remain on your knees in prayer.

The Lord will never forsake us in difficult times. Life itself is a school of learning, and God has provided both a Savior and help to see us through it—the Holy Spirit. We do plan our ways, but truly it is the Lord who directs our steps. We live in a world where sin has dominion, where things happen contrary to our best plans. People disappoint us. Plans change. Sometimes I've prayed earnestly for the situation or wrong to be righted; in the end, I've learned to say, "Okay, Lord, if this is what You are asking of me, I need Your help, Your wisdom, Your perseverance to help me find my way through this." I can honestly say it doesn't always happen overnight, in a week, a month, or year. But once I relinquish it to the Lord, I find a strength to pick up and go on. Instead of saying or thinking, *Why me?* I came to realize he didn't promise me a rose garden without thorns. He promised in John 15 to prune me.

Leona's manifest purpose was to live life as a testimony to God's faithfulness. She believed that our life has enduring significance and that Christians have an eternal purpose for their lives. She shows us how to lay up treasures in heaven and serve the Lord's purposes here and now. It is easy to profess head knowledge of this precept, but to acquire heart knowledge is far more difficult. That's why God provides forefathers and foremothers in the faith.

Once in a very difficult time in my life, I wondered how much more I could handle. Deep in prayer and no doubt bewailing what was going on in my life, the Lord began to bring scriptures to mind. Isaiah 55:8 reminded me my thoughts were not his thoughts and his ways were not mine. Clear as a bell, he said, "I know you love Me, and My paths are trying, but I am shaping you, and sometimes you must be broken, for I have a plan and a purpose."

My response was, "O God, help me to bring glory to You! Help me to be Your arms, Your hands, and Your feet!"

"O child, why else have I allowed you to experience so much? For an *empty* vessel cannot be poured out."

I found this note tucked in my recipe box. Indeed, it has been my recipe for life. Some days I am amazed to see how God has used me.

Most pleasant are Leona's letters in which the dossier of her writer's training blends with the matters on her mind and heart. She finds ways to stretch a metaphor until it squeaks and brings a lightness and charm to the recounting of the everyday acts of serving the Lord.

Praise the Lord, we are down to one runny nose, and the laundry is caught up. Six sick people of various ages and stages is a challenge. It gave me a new appreciation for automatic washers and dryers. How far we have come from the wringer-type washers, the long clotheslines stretched between trees or poles and the forked stick we used to hold up the lines hoping they wouldn't break—but how fresh they smelled when we brought them in. Fabric sheets can't hold a candle to that.

My old-fashion "theology" has kept me through many stormy times, but there is a peace that passes understanding and allows me an empathy to someone struggling with heartaches or burdens today.

No wonder Paul encouraged them and us to put on the whole armor of God in Ephesians 6:10–13:

Finally my brethren, be strong in the Lord and in the power of His might. Put on the whole armor of God that you may be able to stand against the wiles of the devil. For we do not wrestle against flesh and blood, but against principalities, against powers, against the rulers of darkness of this age… Therefore take up the whole armor of God that you may be able to withstand in the evil day and having done all, to stand.

What a strange world we live in today. We used to know the difference between right and wrong. Now it is labeled the new morality, and our liberal churches are condoning it. It's a little like the clotheslines we stretched as tight as we could, but the weight of the wet clothes had to be propped up to keep them from dragging in the dirt or grass.

So our faith is stretched by the weight of our burdens for those we love who need to know the Christ who washed away the dark stains of sin and gave us his Holy Spirit to hold us up. The old hymn filters through my thoughts:

What can wash away my sin? Nothing but the blood of Jesus. What can make me whole again? *Nothing* but the blood of Jesus.

What a wonderful beautiful cleansing power there is in the Christ whose blood covers us today.

The reality of the everyday resonates with the practical beauty of the Spirit-filled life. Leona brings a clear-eyed, forthright, fearless assessment to the most central of human relationships—that of marriage and family life. Only eighteen on her wedding day, she seems to have known early—instinctively—that the ordinary calling of marriage and family are to be committed to the Lord's rule and care.

Her cherished hope is to build a family—faithful, useful, united in Christ.

> I thought back to the day we were married. After I made Jesus Lord of my life, I never made a conscious decision without first praying about it. That day, the Spirit asked me if I was sure this was what I wanted. I said yes and made a vow that with God's help, I would be a good wife. I did not take a Christian family into that marriage, but I took Jesus; and before I went to bed, I knelt and prayed. My husband honored my love for the Lord, and eventually, children came and grew up knowing a love of their own for God, putting him first in their lives. There were times we made tough decisions. Hardship, illness, heartache, heartbreak—we live in a real world, not a fanciful dream world, and learned the truths of Scripture. We did the best we could, but it was the Lord that sustained us over and above all that life brings.

The same steadfast defense of the family and faith sustained Leona in a time of great concern and eventual heartbreak for her church family, for the church at large, and for the nation. Over the years, Dodge Memorial Church's denominational affiliations moved from the congregational communion to the United Church of Christ. Formed in 1957, the United Church of Christ as a denomination trends to a liberal theological position on social and cultural issues. Though member congregations are independent in matters of doctrine and ministry and may not always adhere to the General Synod's theological polity, it was clear to Leona that Dodge Memorial, the church where she was led to Christ, the church where she raised her children, was aligned with the UCC Synod in its position on the ordination of ministers in relation to sexual orientation. In the mid-1990s, she carried on a vigorous and articulate correspondence with the UCC, objecting to its policy without success. There is an unmistakable sense of sorrow for this denouement.

> I am thankful to God for the church my children grew up in and the wonderful people who helped train them up to love God, for the friends I made and still have there. It was not the church but the doctrine of men I could no longer support. We live in a world of new morality. It has had its impact on those churches that have allowed it to take a foothold in the denomination, and God has said he will remove its lampstand. He warns when we are neither hot or cold he will spew us out of his mouth (Revelation 3:15–19). We need to pray for our nation and for our leaders, but we can take heart—God knew the end from the beginning and sent his only begotten son that whosoever believeth in him shall not perish but have everlasting life. Hallelujah! Victory is still in God's hands, and we have a story to tell the nations.

The weekly letters become a dialog, the bright-red lipstick of life, the wrinkled smile at the corners of the eyes in the broad sweep of this conversation. We hear once again her voice, rich in spiritual wisdom. She would say,

> It's all about my relationship with the Lord. I give this to you to encourage you on your own walk with the Lord. I give this record to you because what you do counts for eternity. I have confidence in the Lord and in you.

After a thoughtful pause, she might add,

> Habits of faith are an act of the will; they take effort and discipline. Every aspect of your life

is formed by your journey in the Christian faith. Psalm 121 comforts us with the sure knowledge that God keeps us on this journey. Seek with all your heart to practice the Christian virtues taught to us by God's Word. And when you must defend your faith, tell one and all about the loving, true, and faithful things God has done, is doing, and will do. This may be the most lasting and meaningful memorial you leave as a legacy.

I thought when we are young, "forever" seems before us. Then we reach this age and wonder how we got here so quickly. Now I have an urgency to do things. It has nothing to do with my salvation. Rather, it is a feeling of tying up loose ends, of meeting obligations, of spending time with those I love here while looking over the threshold of time to seeing those who have already finished the race. In Psalm 39:4, David said it so wisely: "Lord, make me to know mine end, and the measure of my days, what it is, that I may know how frail I am." David never wanted to lose sight of the fact his days, as all of ours, are numbered.

Jesus went before us to Calvary that our crooked places might be made straight. He went to the grave, overcame it, and returned to his Father while people watched him go. No doubt, no maybe or might have. He did it. Now the way that leads to heaven is before us, for by grace have we been saved. Hallelujah.

CHAPTER 10

Leona's Bible

I am making scones this morning. The recipe calls for flour, raisins, walnuts, lemon zest, culinary lavender, and a whole stick of cold, sweet, unsalted butter cut into pieces. To incorporate the butter evenly in the dough, I use a pastry cutter. It is my mother's pastry cutter, one of the few pieces of her kitchen equipment I salvaged from her last home. The pastry cutter has a wooden handle, and it comes from the age when some kitchen tools have painted decoration. The paint flakes; I am careful to hunt for and remove stray flakes of paint before I begin my work. The handle is familiar and still fits the curve and palm of my right hand. My mother taught me to make pie crusts with this tool, wonderful flaky creations for ten-inch Pyrex pie plates, often filled with sliced apples for a double-crust apple pie or the custard for pumpkin pies—nothing fancy. The recipe from the pumpkin puree can helped me make perfectly silken slices. My sister and I were taught to whip egg whites for lemon meringue pies using a hand egg beater. We cooked fillings for chocolate cream pies and coconut cream pies on the stovetop in a double boiler. To my mother, it was a matter of pride to know how to cook "from scratch." The taste I remember of those unctuous desserts far surpasses the modern-day convenience of opening a can of store-bought fillings. I am proud of the even pea-sized dots of butter scattered throughout my dough; I have the satisfied sense that these scones will please the ones for whom I am baking them.

My mother was a good cook, with skills acquired during a hard-scrabble subsistence in the coal mining hills of western Pennsylvania. She was the eleventh child in a family of twelve children, growing up in a 140-year-old coal miner's shack slumped onto the side of a hill near the West Virginia border. She cooked food on a coal-fired range in the kitchen. One of my mother's chores as a child was to take a burlap sack down to the holla where the train tracks ran to scrounge pieces of coal fallen from the coal cars leaving the mine. Throughout her life, she suffered the arthritic effects of hoisting and hauling those heavy bags of purloined fuel on her back. The first of her family to graduate from high school, she left her beautiful but desperately poor hillside home in 1940—with nothing but that high school diploma—to emigrate to Detroit in search of work. In due time, the country plunged into World War II, and my mother became a Rosie the Riveter, building the nose section of the Boeing B-29 Superfortress bomber in the war-production converted Chrysler DeSoto plant on Warren Avenue. At the end of the war in 1945, she was thrown out of work along with thousands of other war worker women. She took a job as a waitress and eventually as a cook at a diner on the corner of Third and Willis. There she met a young man mustered out of the Army, back home from some of the bloodiest fighting in the Pacific theater of the war on Luzon and Leyte islands in the Philippines.

He was also eleventh in a family of twelve. He did not graduate high school, leaving the one-room school after eighth grade at sixteen years old to work on the family farm in rural northern Michigan near Gaylord. As a child, too young to handle the farm equipment and wrangle the dangerous steers and other stock, he cooked the family meals on a wood-burning range. When the war came, he wasted no time enlisting in the Army and left the farm in the dust of his boots.

And she married him.

Much later, in my early teens, we manage for a few years to take family vacations with my mother in the late summer just before the start of school. We stay in her Appalachian home in that coal miner's shack, thumbtacked to the side of the hill. It is still a matter of pride for my mother, even in the blistering heat of summer, to cook our meals on that coal-fired range in the kitchen, though her two bachelor brothers who now live in the house have installed a more or less modern electric stove. For an entire glorious week with my mother, we sleep upstairs in the ancient iron beds, eat and drink from the original family china, feast on the abundance from the garden, sit in the back porch swing in the evenings, and listen as my mother and uncles retell, with relish, family stories. The passage of time blurs the edges of a tenuous existence in the coal patches of southwestern Pennsylvania. As evening descends to darkness, mists roll down this Pennsylvania holla, fireflies glide in on gossamer curtains of fog, and the unmistakable taste of coal attar is bitter on the tongue. Under the steeply slanted roof upstairs we drift off to dreams in the silence of the hillside without the fearful awakenings from shouts and cursings and sometimes slams and thuds at home. Then we return home. My mother resumes her work schedule, working twelve or thirteen hours a day for seven hour's pay, for as many days a week as she can escape life with her family.

I become the cook at home, holding together the family sustenance. Amid my shortcomings and disappointments that my mother freely expressed to me, there was one thing she never criticized and she sometimes even encouraged—my cooking.

An old-fashioned kitchen tool, just a small insignificant part of a life lived and left behind, but the power of such objects moves us beyond their simple existence, absorbing and reflecting the family life, the family story. What is remembered from that family story, what is kept and preserved leaves a trace of what is important and a revelation of what is valuable. A useful artifact becomes an heirloom, a family treasure, its value measured in people and memories. The shadows cast by the heirloom are a gift, leaving a record of its story so its owner can be more deeply known.

Heirlooms reside in unlikely and even likely places, not just in kitchen drawers but also in attic trunks, in scrapbooks and photo albums, as recipes and cookbooks, collections, and holiday decorations, toys, quilts, jewelry, faded bundles of letters, family Bibles. The life of a family is bound up in heirlooms that lead us to contemplate what loved ones have learned and experienced in life. Heirlooms hold stories; stories become history. Recording and preserving the stories of the past brings compassion for the challenges encountered and an appreciation for the resilience needed to survive adversity—recovery, triumph, and the reclamation of happiness despite hardship. It is a message that you are a part of something bigger than just this moment and that we all have a place in history. It is this history and this sure knowledge that we also will leave heirloom hallmarks that inspire a blessed thankfulness for the past and establish hope for the future.

We walked in the door of Amy's house on a sunny, hot afternoon in Omaha, Nebraska. Amy dropped everything she was doing to prepare for her mother Sandy's eightieth birthday party. She disappeared into a back room of the house, emerging a few minutes later with a large, dark-covered unmistakable Book. Amy, whom I am meeting in person for the first time, placed the large Book gently, reverently, in my hands.

"This is Grandma's Bible. I am sure you want to see it."

I am captured immediately by the sense that this is a precious object, an important artifact in the story of Leona's life—Sandy's mother, Amy's grandmother. More than that, it is an heirloom part of this family's dowry. The same hands that wrote weekly letters laid themselves upon the pages of this Book, drew from this Book comfort and solace, grace and peace. I sensed that I was about to journey down a different path, a bridge to a place in Leona's faith and character as a child of God.

Much later, in the quiet aftermath of the celebration, I sat alone on the front porch swing with Leona's Bible. Family Bibles have become cherished heirlooms in their own right alongside other mementoes of family life. Prior to the American Revolution, Bibles were imported to the colonies from England, produced by licensed publishers. Other European governments also authorized and certified publishers in order to ensure the accuracy of translations and prevent doctrinal error. What seems like unwarranted control will prove wise in the coming century. In 1781, the newly minted United States Congress approved the first American publisher, Robert Aitken, to print his version of the Bible. By the dawn of the nineteenth century, ten thousand copies had been printed. From thence the floodgates opened.

The first organization of major influence in Bible publishing was the American Bible Society, founded in 1816 in New York as a national coalition of state and local Bible societies. Original founders included its first president, Elias Boudinot, who happened to be president of the Continental Congress from 1782 to 1783. Other influential founders included John Jay, first chief justice of the Supreme Court, and Francis Scott Key, who served as vice president of the society for over twenty-five years. The society's goal was simple—to provide a Bible for anyone who did not own one. To achieve this goal, the society initiated efforts called "general supply." By the 1830s, its first general supply had printed over a million Bibles. Among its distribution methods, the society engaged in a technique used by Charles Spurgeon in England—the use of colporteurs. Itinerant Bible salesmen put shoe leather on the ground and traveled throughout the United States, selling or giving away Bibles. Surprising success drove the demand for two more general supply printings by the end of the nineteenth century.

In the 1840s, two hundred different publishers, situated in fifty different cities, produced 350 different Bible versions. It was the biggest single publishing effort of that time. This was still but a small part of the explosion of the religious press producing Evangelical literature that appealed to a broad audience. Easy availability of printed literature ripened into a potent element, driving the Second Great Awakening.

Bibles came in many different shapes, sizes, bindings, and versions. By the mid-1800s, sizes ranged from small, portable versions for travelers to the large quarto or folio formats. The American Bible Society produced "pocket Bibles" for soldiers fighting in the Civil War—on both sides of the conflict. In the 1840s, publishers introduced a widespread practice of textual notes and illustrations, some refined and even lavish. This gave rise to the creation of a Bible genre unto itself—family Bibles, large, heavy, and expensive—intended for display in the parlor of the family's home. Near the end of the century, Bible publishers conceived editions of the Scriptures that were almost Bible encyclopedias, incorporating illustrations, marginal and cross-reference notes, commentaries, and intertextual essays.

But the original intent of the family Bible was that of a large durable almanac designed to record and preserve the family registry for generations to come. Early family Bibles included special pages in the frontispiece for a family tree, but eventually, this became a section inserted in the middle of the Bible between the Old and New Testaments. Family Bibles were sold in stores, available by mail order, but most often were purchased from those door-to-door salesmen, the colporteurs.

The Records or Registry section in the middle of the Bible commonly included pages to transcribe births, marriages, deaths, baptisms, godparents, and church membership. Some included a specially decorated section to construct family genealogy. What most often excites family historians, however, is the other family ephemera tucked into the pages: newspaper clippings, obituaries, funeral cards, marriage licenses, photos, letters, cards, even deeds or wills—remnants of family life. Outside the confines of the of the Registry section are often found handwritten notations in the margins of the text, underlined verses, tattered edges of much-loved sections. The personal essence of family and connection pervades this remnant of family life. Despite such a sacred sense once given to a family heirloom, a strong antiques market exists in which family Bibles are sought after, collected, traded, bought, and sold. How could someone sell one's grandparents' family Bible!

Leona's Bible is a blended version of the personal and the family Bible. At one time on the inside front cover, she began a list of her favorite verses but soon ran out of room. The frontispiece declares: "This Holy Bible is the property of Leona Mae Moats." It is an Authorized (King James) Version, Self-Pronouncing Reference Edition. There is a concordance and at the back a section titled "Bible Study Helps"—articles, essays, comparison tables, word lists, an index and dictionary, and finally, a Bible atlas. This is, therefore, a "cyclopedic Bible," a modern all-encompassing study aid for the Bible student. The copyright date is 1944: "Produced expressly for SEARS, ROEBUCK and Co. by the National Bible Press in Philadelphia. Crystal Clear Type. Printed in USA."

The National Bible Press is a company of some historical depth rooted firmly in the middle of the nineteenth-century Bible-printing fever right from its start, in the northeast part of downtown Philadelphia during the Civil War years. The National Bible Press's claim to distinction is that of long-time publisher for Gideons International, an organization itself begun by traveling salesmen who became colporteurs for the Lord. National Bible Press Bibles, as part of the Gideons movement, found places in hotel rooms, hospitals, medical offices, military bases, colleges, and prisons. After long and distinguished service, producing over a billion Bibles from its inception in the 1860s, National Bible Press closed its doors in Philadelphia in 2019, moving its production facilities to Crawfordsville, Indiana, as part of LSC Communications. The thought is mildly amusing that Leona made a trip to her local Sears, Roebuck and Co. store to purchase the Christian artifact which meant the most to her—the Holy Scriptures.

Leona's Bible was a *working* Bible. Verses are underlined, notes take up space in the margins, page corners are bent as markers. In the tradition of the family Bible format, she has recorded her marriage to Ronald Charles Moats on July 24, 1939. There are lists of children and grandchildren and their spouses. There are the births and decease dates for brothers and sisters, parents and grandparents. If there had been more extensive pages provided for a family tree, Leona would have traced her colonial and pioneer heritage to Daniel Boone and Noah Webster Jr. Daniel Boone is Leona's great-great uncle through her grandfather George McClelland Butcher. Noah Webster Jr.—the distinguished teacher, essayist, and publisher of the *American Dictionary of the English Language* (1828)—is a distant relative through her grandmother Nettie Webster Butcher's lineage. A poignant reminder caps the pages of Leona's Bible: "Honor thy father and thy mother" (Exodus 20:12). Tucked in between these pages are newspaper clippings from the *Omaha World Herald*, bookmarks, pages torn from devotional tracts, the bulletin from Leona's funeral service. The family Bible becomes the safest place for the most important heirlooms of life. So well-used was this cherished Book that as a gift one Christmas, her son-in-law Bill, Sandy's husband, had its tattered cover removed and the entire text rebound at Capital Bindery in Omaha.

I imagine Leona bent over this Book reading and studying by lamplight, the sun's faithful promise brightening the skies outside the screenhouse by the Missouri River, the first tentative birdsongs in glorious companionship. The weight of her Bible in my hands brought a momentary sense of fulfillment accorded only by things that can be touched, things that can be handled by us and by special others, loved ones beyond the eyes, even beyond the voice, special things connect us to loved ones, a sublime union, a unity of spirit. It may be as simple as a pastry cutter or as recondite as a Bible. As

Leona's hands turned these pages and my hands come after, grace abounds and proceeds, a blessed gift.

"She was an old-school Evangelical," remembers The Reverend Jeffrey B. Wilson, Leona's grandson-in-law. It is a phrase he speaks with warmth and affection. "She was traditional in her devotion to Scripture, Bible study, and prayer. She lived out her faith in the works and activities she dedicated to the Lord."

Leona's love for the Scriptures is unmistakable in her letters. In her own accounts of her conversion experience, she is drawn into the Word almost from the moment she believed. From this time, she watched others value God's Word, and she observed their strivings to live by God's Word. The Spirit infused her heart with reverence and respect for the Word, and it took a deep and abiding root in her soul. I turned the pages alongside the person whose family Bible it was, who believed with her whole heart in reconciliation, redemption, and forgiveness, whose reverence for God's Word was the standard by which she lived, dependent upon the grace, mercy, and lovingkindness of God. She understood clearly the vital tenet of the Scriptures: love the Lord with all your heart, mind, soul, strength and your neighbor as yourself. It is a place from which to begin conversations with God, and it became a place from which to begin conversations about God, spreading the good news of salvation.

Being "old school" signifies a connection to the past formed by heritage and practice. Along with Evangelicals, Leona's life bore the sure signs of a personal and emotional connection in religious affections, an individual response and responsibility. She believed that God speaks plainly in his Word, and it is to be understood simply and applied to the Christian's life. The faith so mercifully supplied by the Savior requires action, serving Christ in works and deeds. Leona had an original way of describing this work in her letters: "putting feet to my prayers." I find in those letters a magnetic, marvelous picture of the passion and motivation for her Christian living and service. Her service to the Lord—more than eighty years—has its historical origin in the development of Christianity in the heartland of our country.

But what gave strength and energy to her convictions expressed in her Christian walk? The enduring practices of Evangelicalism. To be "old-school Evangelical" carries an intriguing connection to the history and culture of religious development, from the profound influences in the 1500s in Europe and the Reformation to pre-Revolution America.

The seed of Evangelicalism is traced through the religious ardor kindled in the late seventeenth century. The stirrings began in the Lutheran church as a growing movement called Pietism. Pietism stressed an experiential focus of conversion, particularly an individual response in faith and a sensitivity to the workings of the Holy Spirit. A literal, personal reading of the scriptures accompanied the striving for holy living. Among those affected by the Pietist movement was John Wesley who, along with his brother Charles and George Whitefield, formed the Holy Club at Oxford in England. Wesley founded the club for prayer, study of the Scriptures, and encouragement in the pursuit of a "devout Christian life" with particular attention to "inner holiness." It was expected that members give proof of a period of spiritual struggle, concluding with a convincing conversion experience. The group was kindly known as the "Oxford Methodists" for their structured religious practice. Some observers, less generous in their characterization, called them religious fanatics. Ordained as ministers, John Wesley preached, Charles Wesley preached and more famously wrote hymns, but it was George Whitefield who sparked the embers of revival in the 1730s and the Great Awakening,

Whitefield began preaching to large crowds in Bristol and London in England. A theatrical, dramatic style incited the audience's emotional response to the simple message of the necessity of conversion. In February 1739, Whitefield began preaching outdoors to accommodate the crowds drawn to his preaching. By May of the same year, he was preaching to crowds of over fifty thousand people, outdoors, in the "open air." It was the birth of revivalism.

Across the ocean in America, revival broke out in 1734 under the preaching of Jonathan Edwards. Late in 1739, Whitefield made his way across the Atlantic Ocean to New England, exhorting at churches and open air events, adding his energy to the movement in the States. Whitefield was now known to make a simple entreaty at the end of his sermon: "Come poor, lost, undone sinner. Come just as you are to Christ."

The spirit of the Great Awakening and its inflamed religious ardor slackened by the mid-1740s, but a smoldering interest in intense emotional religious experience remained. During this time, conflicts and schisms erupted within Protestant denominations, between those who supported revivalism, termed "new school," and those opposed to the new practices, the "old school." Old-school orthodox belief and reliance upon learned, historic theology, liturgy, and church tradition was challenged by a persistent clamor to reach the "common man." What was at first a subtle reconstruction of Christian belief and practice became a waterfall flowing swiftly and rather erratically toward a diverse, popular culture approach to theology. The value of the "individual conscience" and "personal experience" was foremost. The new-school disciples "taught that divine insight was reserved for the poor and humble rather than the proud and learned." The new-school preachers, many of them untrained, uneducated, poor, and humble themselves brought youthful exuberance, pulpit storytelling, intimate personal experience, fervent appeals, and even folksy and sometimes raffish humor to revival preaching. The thousands of their hearers of "low estate" accepted the gospel lifeline thrown to them. The powerful, appealing preaching deeply affected those who heard it. The emotional ardor, as a result, inspired a renewed involvement in religious exercises. Believers and seekers alike were roused to read and interpret the Scriptures for themselves.

At the conclusion of the upheaval known as the American Revolutionary War, the new republic again turned to spiritual matters and a great concern for spiritual renewal. The Second Great Awakening gained a foothold in the early 1800s, gathering with it the still-hot embers of the Great Awakening. A quest to apply the rudiments of democracy and an emerging taste for self-determination in all things united with the irresistible appeal of personal, emotional religious experience.

Westward expansion, inaugurated by the Louisiana Purchase in 1803 and expressed in the cultural mission of Manifest Destiny, had a profound impact on religious practice. As settlers spread westward, vast areas of the country were sparsely settled. In time, the vast western regions developed the civilized and communal life of the towns and cities that settlers left behind in the east. Thousands of pioneers moved into and made new homes and settlements in the wide-open territories. There were few churches. Mainline churches in the east—Congregationalists, Presbyterians, Episcopalians—with clergy in established, comfortable positions had little interest in uprooting and moving to the rough, lean west. The pioneers who left such churches with their highly educated clergy and the traditional Calvinist forms of worship sought religious experiences in line with the excitement and challenges of the limitless frontier.

It was but a matter of time. Revival broke out in 1800 in Logan, Kentucky, led by James McGready, a Presbyterian minister, at the Red River Meeting House. Several hundred people attended this meeting, the first of what became known as the "camp meeting." The gathering at least afforded an opportunity to forsake the isolation and hard life in the wilderness for a few days of fellowship. Instead, religious fervor took over. In 1801, Barton Stone and Alexander Campbell, also Presbyterian ministers, led the Cane Ridge Revival at the Cane Ridge Meeting House in Paris, Kentucky, north and east of Logan. Over the six-day series of meetings, an estimated twenty thousand people, of Presbyterian and Methodist worshiping communities in the backwoods, drew near to the event for an annual communion service. Among those attending was Peter Cartwright, a Methodist circuit rider and missionary, known as the "Backwoods Preacher" and the "Lord's Plowman." Ordained by Francis Asbury in 1806, Cartwright rode circuits in Kentucky, Illinois, Tennessee, Indiana, and Ohio for fifty years. Methodist circuit riders took the fire and fervor of the revival across the vast areas opening for settlement. Francis Asbury, ordained by John Wesley in England in 1767, traveled to Philadelphia in 1771 and began his circuit riding and Methodist missionary work in the colonies at the age of twenty-two. We know much of life on the frontier because of a journal kept by

Asbury in which he described the frontier life on his travels with detailed descriptions of settlements and villages.

Few circuit riders were as educated as Cartwright or Asbury. Most were unschooled, sometimes self-appointed itinerant ministers who, nevertheless, were moved by their genuine zeal and love for the Lord. This common-sense and "common man" association appealed to the hardworking settlers, who brought with them disdain for educated, high-church eastern ministers and the cold, formal structure of Presbyterian and Congregational polity. Along with the plain preaching of the circuit riders came access to copies of the Scriptures, tracts, and spiritual newspapers tailored to the growing revivalist scene. The American Bible Society began publishing the King James Version of the Bible in 1816, and from there, the access to religious literature became key in the spread of the Second Great Awakening. The availability of printed materials designed to appeal to the layman religious seeker let every man read, consider, and decide upon religious matters for himself. Evangelical preachers were quick to sense the advent of mass communications, an efficient way to broadcast the truth of the gospel. The variety and especially the quantity of printed materials increased: newspapers, pamphlets, tracts, spiritual songbooks, and hymn books, and journals became a virtual flood of Evangelical literature. By 1830, the American Tract Society, the first company to have a Treadwell Press, printed over six million tracts annually. From that point forward, the power of the printed word was applied by nearly every denomination and religious society—from John Wesley and the Circuit Riding preachers to the Seventh-Day Adventist print shop and the prolific writer Ellen G. White. Combine this with the irresistible promise of the emotionally engaging religious experience, and the country was poised for a new birth in which prominent evangelists stir the fires of religious enthusiasm.

Charles Grandison Finney intended to become a lawyer. A dramatic conversion experience led him in an altogether different direction. Convinced of a call to ministry, he began theological studies under George Washington Gale, the Presbyterian minister of the church Finney attended, in order to become a licensed minister. Not long into his studies, some misgivings and disagreements arose between him and the doctrines of the Presbyterian Church, and he struck out on his own as an itinerant preacher. In his early work, he led revivals in the Rochester area of western and central New York in 1824, also known as the "Burned-over District." This region was home to an extraordinary degree of religious activity and formation of new religious movements such as the Millerite Movement and the beginnings of Ellen G. White's work. As momentum for Finney's brand of revivalism grew, he preached in larger cities including New York, where he became pastor of Second Free Presbyterian Church. Finney's methods in revival meetings brought criticism down upon him, for he embraced what he called the "New Measures" in revival preaching. He spoke extemporaneously with dramatic and intense but simple language, intending to elicit emotional responses from his listeners. What drove him was the fervent belief that the sinner must "feel religion," and the best way to do that was through preaching in the language of "common life," making it audience-centered. At the front of the hall, an anxious bench awaited those who were experiencing either deep conviction or doubt. Women were allowed to participate and to pray aloud in these meetings, and new converts were urged—or rushed—into church membership. His methods reaped opposition and criticism from old-school Presbyterianism, which held grave concern that the methods brought on shallow-minded fanaticism. But support for Finney and his methods was unmistakable, and he was regarded as the informal leader of new-school Presbyterianism and the free-church movement. By the end of his career in the late 1860s, in some circles he was accorded the title "Father of American Revivalism."

But there was more to come. The Great Revival of 1857, also known as the Third Great Awakening, swept through Chicago. Counted among the converts was a young businessman who sold shoes—D. L. Moody. He was born into a large impoverished family in 1837 in Northfield, Massachusetts. As a young boy, he was sent away from his family to work for food. There was little opportunity for education, but his mother insisted upon faithful church attendance. At the age of seventeen, he found work at an uncle's shoe store in Boston, where he attended his uncle's church. There he had a powerful conversion experience that thrust him into a career as an evangelist.

Moody moved to Chicago in 1856 to start his own shoe business, which became prosperous and enabled him to begin evangelistic pursuits, activities, that satisfied his heart. He started a Sunday school that eventually served over one thousand orphans, poor, and abused children. He became a full-time preacher in 1860 and organized the Illinois Street Church, known as the Moody Memorial Church, (still in existence today). The Civil War erupted in 1861, and Moody went to the battlefields, serving as a minister in the field to both Union and Confederate soldiers.

Moody had limited education, but he was known as a student of the Bible. He preached with enthusiasm, with Finney's persuasion of "plain talk" for the common man. Eventually, he traveled throughout the United States, England, and Scotland, speaking to throngs of seekers, even in such places as Charles Spurgeon's Metropolitan Tabernacle in London in 1875. He brought a new wrinkle to evangelistic meetings, one which would become an important feature for revivalists in the future—the use of music. Ira D. Sankey was an amateur gospel singer and composer when he was recruited by Moody. Sankey's musical contributions to Moody's evangelistic programs introduced the emotional connections brought about by music as well as an attractive element of entertainment.

Moody's legacy is profound. The vast realm of Moody's service and influence in the late nineteenth century remains with us today. Religious historian James Findlay calls him the "creator of modern mass revivalism." After starting Sunday schools for children, Moody's energies and vision carried him beyond the formation of Moody Memorial Church to Moody Bible Institute and, eventually, to broadcast and print ministries. Moody Press began in 1886 as the Colportage Association, and students of the Moody Bible Institute used horse-drawn wagons to distribute the low-cost tracts and religious books. Children, the poor, and lost sinners were always on Moody's heart.

As revivalism drew to a close at the end of the nineteenth century, new threats emerged in the evangelical world. Higher criticism

and the growing attention to Darwinian Theory created contro-
versies which consumed the energy of the church and gave rise to
Fundamentalism, a reaction to these challenges. The ensuing debates
consumed more than a quarter century. By the end of Moody's life
in 1899, the Evangelical-modernist dispute asserted its place in the
outlook for religious activity into the twentieth century.

The revivalist impulse, however, did not dissipate entirely; it
reemerged from the most unlikely places. Billy Sunday, baseball
player-turned-evangelist, was also a son of poverty. Born to a large
family in a log cabin in 1862 in Iowa, his mother was forced to send
her children to the Soldier's Orphans Home for food and shelter.
Sunday's love of sports and athletic ability gave him a pathway out of
poverty. He signed on to play professional baseball for the Chicago
White Stockings in 1883. It was in Chicago one afternoon that
Sunday happened upon a street corner preaching team of the Pacific
Garden Mission (still the oldest continuously operating rescue mission in the United States) and experienced a powerful conversion. It
was the hymns being sung—music—the same hymns he heard his
mother sing that riveted his attention and drew him to the preaching.
Sunday became involved with the YMCA and its work and accepted
a position as assistant secretary in 1891, leaving baseball for good.
His work for the next three years for the "Y" involved many pastoral
kinds of duties, perfect preparation for the next step in his career.
In 1893, he became full-time assistant to J. Wilbur Chapman, who
enjoyed renown as an evangelist in the 1890s. This apprenticeship
prepared Sunday to take up the reins of revival preaching. Known for
a plain spoken, homespun, sometimes coarse preaching style with a
frenetic delivery, he was, nevertheless, popular and productive, gar-
nering some wealth as a result of his work. Eventually he campaigned
throughout the United States, first in large cities then smaller towns,
until his work declined in popularity in the 1920s. Over the length
of his career, the self-proclaimed "old fashioned preacher of the old-
time religion" may have preached to more than one hundred million
people.

Beyond the debates of Higher Criticism and evolutionary theory, the world at large in the early twentieth century was transformed

by rapid political, social, and cultural changes stoked by two World Wars. The shadow of revivalism materialized as a new religious awareness with an urgency to spread the gospel, reach the unconverted, and establish an involvement in the human needs of society rather reminiscent of Moody's work. Evangelicalism was shaken and sifted by the clamorous expansion of Fundamentalism. The timing was perfect for a unifying voice in the progress of the gospel with Fundamentalist tenets—Billy Graham, whose work covered six decades of evangelistic crusades with an undeniable focus on mass conversions.

Graham graduated from Wheaton College in 1943. He spent the first two years of his ministerial life quietly as the pastor of a Baptist church in Illinois. Then he was hired as the first full-time evangelist by Youth for Christ, which was looking for "dynamic young evangelists using revolutionary methods, conducting lively mass rallies" across the United States. He traveled the US in 1945 through 1946 and all over Europe in 1946 through 1947, gaining valuable experience conducting large crusades. In the fall of 1947, Graham decided to strike out on his own. He developed a schedule of citywide crusades in America. The very first citywide crusade was held for one week in Grand Rapids, Michigan, in September 1947, drawing a total of six thousand people. Buoyed by this modest success, Graham's next commitment was November 1947 in Charlotte, North Carolina. Different from his "youth rally" approach in Grand Rapids, Graham tested another program in Charlotte, ending up with what was termed a mix of "gospel variety show and traditional revival meeting." As he continued to build his lineup of campaigns, he began to refine the programs and methods, developing the "art" of revival meetings: powerful preaching, choirs for music to stir the emotions, and the invitation to come forward to receive Christ. Such "inquirers" met one-on-one with counselors, who answered questions and prayed with the supplicant. In what became a trademark of the invitation, a musical performance of Charlotte Elliott's 1835 hymn "Just As I Am" accompanied those going forward. Having made the decision early on to include music, Graham hired George Beverly Shea and song leader Cliff Barrows, who both became an enduring part of the program. Graham seemed to sense the emotional connection created by music, not unlike Billy Sunday and even D. L. Moody. By the September 1949 crusade in Los Angeles that was initially scheduled for three weeks but stretched astonishingly for eight weeks in circus tents in a downtown parking lot, Billy Graham established himself in the Evangelical world in an extraordinary way. In 1950, Graham consolidated his expanding ministry with the organization of the Billy Graham Evangelistic Association. Outreach eventually involved magazines, radio and television broadcasts, a resource library described as "an ongoing crusade," and, not surprisingly, Internet evangelism. Billy Graham's indefatigable presence and labor for God on the world stage resulted in more than four hundred revival crusades worldwide from 1947 through 2005.

Considering the history of the Evangelical religious endeavor, evidence is compelling that "large meetings and mass conversions" kept the Evangelical movement going forward in the twentieth century. It is a noble work that accents the renewal of the heart and the vitality of the Christian religion, and it left a legacy: Christian belief and the practice of religion is for the layman. Read and understand the Bible for one's self; trained theologians and clergy are not needed to interpret it. The outgrowth of this perspective includes the flourishing of independent churches, foreign mission agencies, Bible colleges, a vast supply of popular literature, scores of radio stations, television programming, and worldwide media presence.

Three hundred years of religious history. The pace of religious and cultural change in the twenty-first century testifies to a new transformative element in Evangelicalism—a call for the return to the Pietist spirituality of the Great Awakenings—personal devotion, holy living, and genuine spiritual experience, living in ways that demonstrate faith from the heart. Contemporary expression of these beliefs is found today in the Emergent Movement, reflecting back to those independent, democratic desires of self-determination and populism that propelled the Second Great Awakening in America. New religious traditions arise as experimentation with different forms of Christian fellowship embrace the community church movement, the house church movement, and the megachurch movement.

Historians seeking to label these new developments call this the era of Postmodern Evangelicalism.

To be known as an "old-school Evangelical" is to but scratch the surface of church history. Taking the time to unravel the past permits a greater understanding of a vast and plain old rich record of Christian religious gumption. To glean from history God's magnificent care of his church in every time and place inspires us in our own pursuit of living in faithful obedience to God. When we look into Leona's life, we observe the influences shaping her Christian walk; and in that walk, we marvel at the exertions that embody a life of faith. We see plainly the practice of drinking deeply from "the hidden springs of communion with God" in the Bible, which sustains the pilgrim through times of declension and suffering. We are comforted and inspired to endure the trials faced in the progress of the spiritual life, giving praise to the Spirit's faithful and creative ways to draw us along the path of the Christian walk. We see the gospel at work in all times and in all places and rejoice in the power of God. We see the gospel at work in others: prominent figures in church history as well as in the everyday common man and in the everyday common woman raising a family, working to support it, living in loving communion with and committed to the cause of serving the church, living a life of obedience to Christ in a distinctly anti-Christian world—the hand of God in the life of a faithful though flawed human servant, as are all of us. In it we see God's providential work wherever history roams. If that is "old-school Evangelical," I want to be one too.

Leona leaves her heart on the page of one of her letters, quoting from the Scriptures in her Bible, as a tribute to her family:

> If I had one legacy to leave my family, it would be found in Luke 6:35–38: But love your enemies, and do good and lend, hoping for nothing again; and your reward shall be great, and ye shall be children of the Highest: for He is kind unto the unthankful and to the evil. Be ye therefore merciful, as your Father also is merciful. Judge not, and ye shall not be judged; condemn

not, and ye shall not be condemned; forgive, and ye shall be forgiven. Give and it shall be given unto you, good measure, pressed down, and shaken together, running over... For with the same measure ye mete out it shall be measured to you. My most earnest prayer this day is for God to bring a Revival such as we have not seen, that will sweep across our nation.

CHAPTER 11

The Seed Sown on Good Ground

Being drawn into a study of church history and then by extension into world history provided an unexpected benefit—it quickened my own soul. I suspect that we live our day-to-day lives in a realm too small, with the depths of our thoughts too shallow. The world may expect us to believe that the course of humanity moves inexorably without pattern or design. The Scriptures teach us differently. History is meaningful, for it has a purpose and a point for our lives. God will bring his purposes to pass, surely and completely, for he rules over history and has decreed all that takes place according to his will:

> In Him also we have obtained an inheritance, having been predestined according to His purpose who works all things after the counsel of His will, to the end that we who were the first to hope in Christ should be to the praise of His glory (Ephesians 1:10–12 NKJV).

Our faith goes with us wherever we go as we take our place in this historical process. Wherever God has placed us, we give witness to his saving work through Christ, making his invisible kingdom visible. We take the ministry and mercy modeled by Jesus to the needy around us—the least of his brethren—and thereby serve God in grateful obedience.

Every Christian needs God's daily sustaining grace to go forth to serve him. The godly living of those who have tread the trail of faithfulness before us is a comforting and salutary gift. As we run the race that is set before us in the Christian life, their examples galvanize our energies and instruct us in the pathways of faith. In light of the great history of the church, the sweeping host of witnesses who lived and died for the faith before us might seem far removed from our own daily struggles to be faithful to Christ. But God provides witnesses all around us today, a gracious provision of his encouragement to go forth to serve him. That was what drew me to Leona, whose example of personal piety was a manifestation of the Savior's favor and goodwill. She was devoted to the Word, to prayer, and to works that attest to a dynamic faith—a loving and beloved child of God.

Pioneer migration westward, the immigrants, both desperate and hopeful, began in earnest after the Louisiana Purchase of 1801. Inspired by the democratic independent egalitarian spirit of the country, thousands loaded all they owned into wagons and headed west. The Homestead Acts and later the California Gold Rush nourished the desire to claim a stake in America's abundance of land and wealth. The only practical means of travel was overland, and in time the Emigrant Trails carried a half million colonizers westward. One of those trails, the Mormon Trail, may have been the most productive of the westward expansion trails, and it originated in Council Bluffs. The Council Bluffs and Omaha area became an influential part of the migration, for it was there that the most commodious crossing of the Missouri River was feasible. So important was the area that it garnered the attention of President Abraham Lincoln, who visited the region in 1859. Despite the impending threat of Civil War, Lincoln was a man of the Midwest, and he had a vision for America. The country's expansion to the shores of the Pacific Ocean was an imperative part of it. Lincoln decided that Council Bluffs would become the eastern terminus of the visionary transcontinental railroad, later formalized in the Pacific Railroad Act of 1862. An observant man, Lincoln may have been persuaded by the fact that one particular emigrant band had already built five river crossings with ferries besides. The Mormons, on their way westward, fleeing religious persecution in the east, left a significant, intriguing, and, as it turns, out pivotal contribution to western settlement.

Before there was Council Bluffs, there was Kanesville. Thomas Kane, attorney, abolitionist, and US military officer met members of Brigham Young's church at a conference in Philadelphia in 1846. Kane had a heart for the oppressed and offered to help the church in its many conflicts with the United States government, as the church sought to find religious freedom in the west. He negotiated a section of land for the Mormons to occupy on the Missouri River. As families moved to the area and began a small settlement, they named it Kanesville in his honor. In return, Kane brokered for the government the organization of the Mormon Battalion as a unit in the US Army, an all-volunteer unit of about 130 soldiers who served from 1846–1847. This service was in exchange for government help, for the Mormons planned migration to Great Salt Lake Valley. The unit fought in the Mexican-American War and eventually marched two thousand miles all over the southwest to California. The far-reaching effect of this journey opened up wagon routes to California and made possible westward expansion to Utah, Nevada, and Arizona. Meanwhile, back at Winter Quarters, a temporary settlement in Kanesville, the Mormons were industrious: over a period of seven years, the Grand Encampment of Mormon Pioneers built a mill, print shops, three hundred houses, hotels, stores, cleared fields, planted crops, and built a tabernacle in nearby Miller's Hollow. In 1851, the leadership heard the call to head west to Great Salt Lake Valley. By 1853, 46 wagon trains, 2,900 wagons, and 25,000 pioneers left it all behind in Kanesville. Not long after, what was left of the town changed its name back to Council Bluffs.

Council Bluffs, Iowa, and Omaha, Nebraska, remain a "cradle of civilization" in the heartland of the Midwest. Lincoln's railroad flourished as Council Bluffs and Omaha became, at one time, the largest railroad hub in the world. The surrounding prairies and their products and presence still speak as a polestar of the rich abundance of America. With it came a reputation for the earnest, hardworking, common-man character based on honest everyday labor done most often with one's own hands. It is a perfect description of the pioneers and the generations thereafter, a fertile soil of the heart found by the revivalists in the Second Great Awakening. Into this great history is born Leona "Grandma" Moats.

If faith is genuine, good works will abound as evidence. Leona learned as a young Christian, by the example of her grandmother and mother, to serve the Lord with good works in gratitude for his inestimable gift of redemption. The seed of faith planted in her heart was sown on good ground, profitable ground, profoundly fruitful ground.

A young working mother in working man's Council Bluffs, she lived across the alley from Dodge Memorial Church. It was her husband's church, and beginning with her marriage in 1940, it became her church for the next thirty-five years. Leona and Ron started out married life in a small apartment furnished by Ron's parents, and eventually, they bought a small modest home nearby.

Leona discerned the needs of the neighborhood in which she lived. She began a ministry, pulling a small wagon, visiting shut-ins and the indigent. She delivered cookies, puzzles, sometimes a bit of literature, and comfort. In essence, she was a modern-day colporteur. Finding a reassuring reception, she expanded to more neighbors who welcomed her encouragement and companionship. At Christmastime, there was hot chocolate, caroling, and more cookies in the neighborhood. As her experience and courage grew, Leona stepped forward more boldly at work, leading Bible studies and prayer meetings at lunchtime. Her church, however, was her beloved home, and in it she became thoroughly involved.

Dodge Memorial Church was one of the oldest Christian congregations in the Council Bluffs area and a church for whom many members over the years have had a great deal of fondness. Begun as a missionary Sunday school in 1893, by 1900, the congregation formally organized as the People's Union Church with seventeen members. In 1907, the church requested membership in the Council Bluffs Association of Congregational Churches. The church purchased land, bought the former First Congregational Church building, and moved it to the lot. It was rebuilt and rededicated on June 16, 1912 as Dodge Memorial Church, in recognition of a family donation in memory of Nathan P. Dodge's contributions and membership in the church. The program published for the rededication ceremony noted a full day of preaching and worship activities, beginning with a sunrise prayer meeting at 6:00 a.m. and ending with an evening "stereopticon address." Over the next twenty-five years, the Lord blessed the congregation with growth, which allowed for the building of a parsonage and major renovations and additions.

A wonderful artifact survived the moving of the First Congregational Church building—the bell. Forged in the 1860s in Pennsylvania, it made the trip to Council Bluffs by boat into the Atlantic Ocean, across the Gulf of Mexico, up the Mississippi River to the Missouri River to St. Joseph, Missouri. The last leg of the journey was made by horse-drawn wagon to Council Bluffs. The bell was installed in the belfry of the First Congregational Church and made the move with the building to Dodge Memorial's site in 1911. It is rumored to still reside in the building in the church attic, now under the care of the latest worshiping congregation, City Light West Council Bluffs. For the pioneers settling our country and building their homes and communities, their church must have a proper bell, and a bell they certainly had.

In this beautiful history-laden place of worship Leona cast her talents. She led Bible studies and worked Vacation Bible School. She penned a regular column in the church newsletter. Shy and reluctant to be in the spotlight as a "leader," nevertheless, she became the Sunday school superintendent, carrying on that work for sixteen years. Leona wrote children's Sunday school materials and wrote and produced children's Christmas and Easter plays.

Leona's interests and activities reached outside the church as well. The 1960s saw the expansion of the modern-day parachurch movement, at times called the Fourth Great Awakening. An expanding scene of nondenominational churches and community faith groups, it was regarded as a subtle movement in Evangelicalism toward Christian work outside and across denominational lines. The early purposes for these groups was that of new evangelism opportunities and social welfare activities. Leona became involved in Aglow International, traveling to several states for conferences, prayer groups, Bible studies, and care groups. Counted as a part of the parachurch groups, the Billy Graham Evangelistic Association also advanced in its work. In 1964, the Crusade made a stop in Omaha, Nebraska. By this time, some seventeen years after the initial Crusade in Grand Rapids, the revival meetings were well-organized, highly-polished, and in need of hundreds of volunteers to assist the crowds of thousands that attended each night. Leona served as one of the counselors but was unaware that her son was among the inquirers one evening. She learned later that a friend, also a volunteer counselor, witnessed him signing his decision card.

Sometime after 1961, Dodge Memorial became Dodge Memorial Christian Church and later Dodge Memorial United Church of Christ. In these later years, Leona was greatly concerned over the church's theological positions and its drift toward liberalism. Sometime in the 1990s, she left this church and began worshiping at a Nazarene church. In her sunset years, she was found worshiping at her final church home, Harvest Community Church in Omaha.

The sphere of Leona's vibrant life of faith is, for me, an inestimable comfort. As we study God's Word in Hebrews 13, we find a distinct reminder to look at the faithful lives of spiritual leaders of the past. We must take care what and whom we respect and emulate. I am encouraged by one with the strength and energy of her convictions: devotion to the Word, prayer, works that give credence to a vigorous faith. It brings to mind that which the Lord teaches us in the parable of the Sower and the Seeds:

> Listen! Behold, a sower went out to sow. And it happened, as he sowed, that some seed fell by the wayside; and the birds of the air came and devoured it. Some fell on stony ground, where it did not have much earth; and immediately it sprang up because it had no depth of earth. But when the sun was up it was scorched, and because it had no root it withered away. And some seed fell among thorns; and the thorns grew up and choked it, and it yielded no crop. But other seed fell on good ground and yielded a crop that sprang up, increased and produced: some thirtyfold, some sixty, and some a hundred. (Mark 4:3–8 NKJV)

Leona's example of personal piety, the imprint of an old-school Evangelical, is a distinctive mark of grace, an affirmation of the seed sown on good ground. She tells of its fruit:

> If there is a secret to coming through difficult times it can be found in the Word of God. How blessed are all of us who were encouraged by Sunday School teachers to memorize Bible verses. How many times in my life has the truth of Psalm 119:105 been my source of help, strength, or encouragement. Quote: "Thy word is a lamp unto my feet and a light unto my path."
>
> I am eternally grateful to those teachers. One in particular took a very shy little girl and built seeds of faith and trust in our Lord, in the child's life, that has carried me through over seventy years. My grandmother used to talk about a "Crown of Jewels" God has for the faithful.

Surely this teacher has received her crown from the Lord she loved and served as faithful.

I am equally blessed to have those among my friends who had such a wonderful influence over my own children. Some may count their blessings in material things, and I have had mine too. But the real treasure lies in the Biblical principles and influences that shaped my children's lives and joy of joy is bearing fruit today even in the fourth generation.

Most of all we thank God for his Presence in all our lives. For the way he has provided and met every need. Comforted and encouraged all of us to trust him!

May you find that so in your life.

Love you in Christ,
Grandma Moats

CHAPTER 12

Honey on the Sweet Potatoes

Leona's Missouri River Home at Honey Creek

Leona and Ronald moved north of Council Bluffs in 1976 to Honey Creek, a small settlement on the Missouri River. There they lived most of their married life and raised their children. Ronald kept a small fishing boat. Leona had a screenhouse in which to read, write, revel in nature, and pray. Family came and went, filling the trailer home on festive holidays with the joyous gatherings Leona loved.

From this home base, the Moats relished retirement time for camping and fishing trips and treks to the beautiful national parks and wild places in America. When Ronald's health declined, they moved back to Council Bluffs in 1993. In 1995, at the age of seventy-five, Leona bought a little red car and learned to drive. She gave up driving at age 80. Her friend Ann Tholen dubbed her "a good little driver."

For a time, the little red car gave Leona the ability to serve others and meet social needs. Being present in others' lives was as important and vital as the air she breathed. Her great joy was the ongoing fellowship of her community of faith, but most of all, she prized the love and consummate care of her family. Her presence is remembered with enduring affection.

Hi Joyce,

I want to let you know about my relationship with Leona. My name is Wanda Moats and I am married to Leona's nephew John.

I knew Leona (Aunt Lonie) longer than I have known my husband and we have been married 52 years. I attended the same church, Dodge Memorial Congregational Church. I can still see her, in my mind, carrying her bible and with the biggest most welcoming smile on her face standing and visiting with the people in the congregation.

Aunt Lonie was one of the kindest ladies I have ever known. You would feel so comfortable being in her presence, no matter what was on your plate, you knew things would work out after sharing your situation with her. She always had time for people and I am not sure how, she was a busy lady. When my mother passed away in 1982, the funeral was in Renwick, Iowa which was several hours from Council Bluffs where we lived at the time as did Aunt Lonie and Ron. The funeral was in a little country church. I walked down the steps to the gathering room and there sat Aunt Lonie and Uncle Ron. That meant so much to me and again had that feeling that things would be okay. The day for them was, round trip probably seven hours of driving plus a few hours of visiting and attending the funeral. She was so special to me and everybody that knew her.

My husband would receive a birthday phone call every year from the time we left Council Bluffs in 1992 until she was not able to remember all the birthdays. She would call before he went to work in the morning, a great way to start his day. When the phone would ring early in the morning of his birthday he would smile and say "Aunt Lonie." When Lonie sent a card or letter it always started with "Dear Loved Ones."

I just wanted to be more like Aunt Lonie, caring, kind, and loving. She saw the best in everybody and brought out the best in all of us. I think they broke the mold when Lonie was born. There isn't another person like her that I know anyway.

These are a few of my memories of Lonie that will stay with me forever.

Wanda Moats

Years of living exacts its toll. Hardship, suffering, and grief tempers the chambers of faith. Leona knew the grief and sin borne in living and was a steadfast help to someone in need. Another nephew, Jim, recalls with grace and gratitude Aunt Lonie's solicitude:

Hi Heidi and Joyce,

I still have a letter from her to me in my right hand desk drawer, just to remind me of how loved I was by her.

My letter to her shared how much our phone calls and talks had strengthened me during a very difficult time in my life. I shared that she was the one person I'd known that was with me in that way and how much she meant to me and that I was sure her life had made a great difference. I also let her know that her work was complete and that she could let go.

Thanks for helping me remember. The tears in my eyes are reminders of her love and the many years her light kept the path in front of me.

Love
Jim

Another niece presents memories of family gatherings, sound advice, and the personal concern Leona had for others.

Joyce,

My name is Chris Moats, and I'm married to Aunt Lonie's nephew, David Moats. His dad, Carroll Moats was brother to Lonie's husband, Ron.

We received letters at Christmas and on special events such as a birthday or occasional letters of encouragement. One of the statements I remember repeatedly was "Keep praying. Sometimes God is last minute!"

Aunt Lonie's letters were heartfelt and encouraging as she shared stories from her own life as she inspired us to keep trusting in God through the good times and the struggles. She validated us a child of God who were welcome to his promises. She used the letters to teach us to trust in him. Her letters always included a salvation message and bible verses.

In her earlier years her letters were personally written and later on, as it got harder to write, photocopied. I love phone calls, but her letters were a place where her deepest spiritual thoughts were imparted to us, her family. In the days now of texts and emails writing letters is becoming a lost art. That she would sit and take the time to write just to "you" to encourage and show unconditional love was very special to us.

She always made you feel like you were the only person in the room. She lit up when she saw you.

She was always filled with gratitude and positivity.

She loved to host our families at holidays. She had the gift of hospitality.

She exuded her love for Jesus and life with a smile and infectious laugh.

She loved everyone and we loved her!

She really enjoyed conversation around the dinner table. She was non-judgmental.

She made the best holiday goodies for us to nibble on…my favorite were her cherry mash bars. We still talk about that goodie tray! Never seen or tasted another one like it!

She loved family.

She was personal and relational.

When at family gatherings it was Aunt Lonie who led prayer before meals. Even today when we pray we'll ask, "Who's going to be Aunt Lonie?"

Chris

"Who is going to be Aunt Lonie" today? Who picks up the standard she held, the fundamental commitment to prayer emblematic of a Christian's life? Prayer reflects the relationship we have with God; it is an act of worship. It is a privilege but also a duty; a notable characteristic of the saints in the history of the church is their devotion to prayer. The discipline of prayer develops and nurtures obedience, and obedience begets godliness that adorns the Christian life. Leona's examples of prayers suffused her family, working their way deeply into their souls and family ways.

Leona made friends among the household of faith wherever she went. When staying with granddaughter Heidi in Michigan, she attended our church and developed a loving collection of acquaintances. One who became a dear friend, Julie, spent many companionable activities and hours with Leona and remembers most clearly the times and moments in which intercessory prayers were needed for others.

> Grandma could *pray*. I don't exactly know how to describe the prayer. We went to visit a friend's baby who was in the hospital in the NICU. Leona just began praying as we circled the baby's bed, just started talking; words and expressions just flowed. She had a "connection" to Someone she knew well—who he is, what he'll do. There was no pleading, no begging. It was a conversation, well-practiced. She had been talking to Jesus for a long time, and there was so much praise in her prayer. She took us to the Lord. A nurse came in, realized what we were doing, and left us to our ministry of healing, every bit as important as her work.
>
> I've heard a lot of people pray; but I have never heard anyone pray like *that*. It was an experience of being caught up in the Spirit. That kind of prayer comes *from* the Lord—his Spirit work-

ing in her, a vital, strong connection to the mystery of God. God has to give us that.

Julie commends Leona's example of a life of devotion and faith:

> Grandma taught and lived the precept: trust in God. We are not alone in any struggle. Her life experience taught her that hardship and trouble shape you in one way or the other. Grandma leaned on Christ and testified that it is once and for all and for good. Knowing this story may earnestly shape our service to one another and to many others. We may never know the impact as we redeem one another, living as servants to one another. The Lord will use it for his eternal purposes. It's like putting honey on the sweet potatoes.

Leona often ended her letters with this personal note: "You are always in my heart and prayers." How much more profound and precious now is this closing.

Granddaughter Heidi folded Leona into her family's everyday life, especially the raising of three children, when Leona spent time in Michigan. Heidi cherished Leona's influence on Hannah, the oldest great-granddaughter:

> Grandma (Leona) taught Hannah important lessons that only a grandmother like her could teach. People will fail you; Christ will not. Your identity is in Christ, not grades, sports, friends. And the discipline of faith is social and cultural, from one generation to the next, learned at your grandmother's knee.

Granddaughter Amy recalls adventures and memories of life with Leona:

> When I was about ten years old grandma and I got on our bikes and rode to the restaurant in town and ate ice cream sundaes. By the time we were headed back to the trailer where they lived, it was really dark. So there we were riding our bikes in the dark, and grandpa came up in his little Datsun with his headlights on us. He pulled us over, proceeded to put our bikes in the car and drove us home. He was so mad at our independence.
>
> Grandma had the best nails for scratching backs.
>
> I love that grandma got up at about 4 o'clock in the morning and was on her knees praying for all of us every day. She truly was a type of person that knew how to forgive and pray for those who trespass against her.
>
> I took care of grandma on and off for seven years and then I had her full on for three years during dementia. I was with her when she took her last breath. As I birthed her into heaven, she looked like she had just walked straight into heaven and was singing with the angels. It was absolutely amazing.

I came to know Leona at first more from her writing—the letters—than personal comradeship. I was stirred her love for God's Word. She celebrated God's providential care and recognized and thanked God for his faithfulness. She affirmed, with confidence and authority, that God's Word is the foundation and direction for serving him and others.

Gradually I knew her as a friend. She had an engaging kindness, concern, and interest in others. It was an empathy for others' needs and especially for the spiritual condition of their heart, and she was always ready at a moment's notice in prayer.

Most of all, it was manifest grace. She believed that God's grace had been poured out upon her, and it was her responsibility to channel that to others. Over and over I read in the letters that she looked to relieve the burdens of others and that her calling was through action: be "Christ's hands, feet, and heart." She believed that hospitality showed the love of Christ. Tell others about Jesus. Indeed, she loved the church wherever she found it.

My interest in her life and, ultimately, her life story began with the provenance revealed in the letters. There is openness, honesty, discussion of the good *and* the bad. There is humility and abundant reminders and examples, in light of it all, to look for joy. Lean on the promises in God's Word. Take them in, and anoint them to your life. Be attentive to the needs of others, of the household of faith *and* for those outside it. Show mercy, for thereby you serve Christ. Our strength is in Christ, and we live every day leaning on that strength.

Her letters are a form of storytelling, the teaching and exhortation and example I sought all my life. They are unselfconscious, unpretentious, an authentic account of Christ's daily work in us as believers. With simple candor we come to know that the practice of the Christian life requires effort, intention, the right kind of motivation and heart's desire. She shows us how to be sensitive to God's leading and to be engaged in his work wherever we find our circumstances: at home, in our occupations in the world, in our church. In all of this, the marvelous love of her Savior was always on her mind and on the tip of her pen.

The beauty and importance of her writing is its disarming simplicity. She takes Scripture and Bible stories, ponders them, and then sees them in relation to what she has experienced in life's joys and trials and toils. She invites us into the realm of her walk of faith as she considers joys and testings "in the chambers of my heart." Her relationship with *her* grandmother and her grandmother's faith left a deep impression upon her. Her lasting legacy is this—to love the Lord and to love the Lord's family brought into your life wherever you find it. Why should we care about Leona? We should care that she is remembered by family and friends and now by new friends as faithful and true to her Savior. We should reach out and receive the baton she passes in the race of this life of faith and run mindful of the model of her endurance. These are the values she lived by that guided and sustained her all throughout life and now in which we may all be inspired. What a marvelous life of grace.

Dear Sally:

Home! What a lovely place to be. I came in Saturday evening. But I never feel completely at home until I go to church. Years ago the Lord taught me a wonderful truth. I could take the cares of my life there and give them to God and find peace, joy and love in joining others to sing praises, offer prayers of thanksgiving, and a renewing of the Spirit. What a joy it was to learn the truth of Romans 12:1: I beseech you therefore, brethren by the mercies of God, that ye present your bodies a living sacrifice, holy, acceptable unto God which is your reasonable service.

That didn't make me a holier-than-thou type. No, it encouraged me to live in life the truths the Spirit taught me in his Word. My grandma told me actions speak louder than words. It kept me in constant contact with my Lord because I found "praying without ceasing" (1 Thessalonians 5:17) became a way of life for me. I knew I did not have the ability on my own to comfort, encourage, or give advice. But I called upon the Lord and he enters into every conversation and every prayer that is offered up to him.

When Jesus prayed for us in John 17:15, I pray not that thou shouldest take them out of the world, but that thou shouldest keep them from evil, he literally asked the Father to go with us into the workplace the shopping centers, the neighbors, and keep us from the temptations.

Romans 12:2: And be not conformed to this world, but be ye transformed but the renewing of your mind, that ye may prove what is that good and acceptable and perfect will of God. I am so thankful that life has been an ongoing school of learning. And the Lord has taken me to the woodshed of obedience on many occasions. But each time faith grew and hope in the life to come kept me looking up. I can truthfully say with Job 23:8–11: We often try every other way but v.10: He knoweth the way that I take, when He hath tried me I shall come forth as gold. My foot hath held His step, His way have I kept and not declined. And Job 19:25: For I know that my Redeemer liveth and He shall stand at the latter day upon earth.

I told my minister once that I hang my problems in the vestibule when I come in and I don't pick them up on the way out.

As the old hymn says: I know whom I have believeth and am persuaded that He is able to keep all that I have committed unto the day when He shall come. As Fanny Crosby wrote in her song, And I shall see Him face to face and tell the story, saved by grace.

Doesn't that make the joybells ring in your heart? We finally got word on Angie. It was not a kidney problem as we feared. But her blood pressure is the culprit. They increased her medicine and gave her a medicine for water retention. It was a trying week, but what a comfort we found in Jesus, and a peace that passeth understanding that kept our hearts and minds through Christ

Jesus. We were comforted and encouraged by all the prayers offered up for all of us and I thank you for praying for us.

P.S.: I got home Saturday night. Went to Al's birthday party Sunday. And am now at my granddaughter's with her son until Friday.

Love you in Christ,
Leona Moats

P.S. As my little great grandson says: God is good. All the time.

AFTERWORD

From the moment we awaken in this world, we become a part of history and embark upon a journey. Many threads form the weaving of the parable of our lives. As Christians, our whole lives are given to the working out of our salvation in the fear and trembling of the Lord:

> For it is God who is at work in you, both
> to will and to work for His good pleasure.
> (Philippians 2:12–13 NKJV)

This is what pleases him. It is not ever simple nor easy. As with most things in this life, the real burdens of living are made lighter through the help and encouragement of those who have already walked this path. How valuable is their history! Reflecting on their past permits us to see the evidence of God's faithfulness. It encourages us in the labor of persevering in the faith. Inspiration develops deep roots when we look upon the lives of the godly who have navigated the seas of this life from the security of the Savior's embrace.

This passage has become for me a sacred journey, a pilgrimage, seeking to know the Lord and to know how to live in right relationship to him. I now recognize the entrance of Leona's letters into my life as a sacramental moment: something precious, something mysterious, sowing the seeds of gratitude and reflection. It turned my heart in a new direction to the Lord, enlarging the possibilities and rewards of a life devoted in service to him.

Looking at Leona's life fulfilled my deep need for a mother in the faith, a touchstone. The Lord placed her in my life just when I needed her spiritually and humanly. The letters led to a story we can all connect to and even have a joyous participation in it. Leona served as my "kinsman redeemer"—one who delivers, rescues, and helps the needy—in the faith. As Leona redeemed me, she served her Savior, who is our ultimate Redeemer. Leona's story gave me cause to rejoice and to persevere in the difficult journey of a Christian life. May this loving tribute to Leona "Grandma" Moats's noble and inspirational story testify to the fruit of the Spirit. With the light of the example of her life, let the path be illuminated as we all endeavor to redeem others and serve our Lord Jesus Christ.

HONEY ON THE SWEET POTATOES: THE LETTERS AND LEGACY OF LEONA MAE "GRANDMA" MOATS SYNOPSIS

LEONA MAE "GRANDMA" MOATS is no ordinary grandmother.

To be sure, Leona led a life disguised as ordinary: growing up in the middle of the western prairies in Council Bluffs, Iowa; attending school (though only through eleventh grade); marrying, working, raising children; attending worship and church activities; but hers was a life filled with extraordinary devotion to the Christian faith. Converted at the age of ten, her faith blossomed with the loving influence of her early church family and the providential care of her devout maternal grandmother.

Leona's childhood was everything the author, Joyce Harlukowicz, did not have growing up. Her home was a place of impoverishment and privation, but the unmerited gift of God's salvation was bestowed upon her in a conversion experience in her late teens. In it the Holy Spirit implanted deep within her heart a hunger for living faithfully to God. Thus began a lifelong quest for guidance in living out the Christian faith. Forty years later, in God's perfect timing, she was brought under Leona's influence through church affiliation and through Leona's distinctive personal practice—letter writing. Leona kept up a weekly letter-writing custom, sending two-page dispatches to more than forty recipients throughout the country. With characteristic grace, Leona adds Joyce to the mailing list.

A writer since her teens, Leona composed weekly two-page letters the last thirty-five years of her life about the joys and challenges of living the Christian faith. The discovery of this ministry reveals a life founded on Christ: her love for the Word of God in the Bible, her love for the music of the church and its hymns, her sage observations on life's testings and the power of prayer, her wisdom evident in comforting, encouraging, and exhorting her readers. In this particular form of narrative, known as commonplacing, we behold the loving and lasting effects of Leona's life upon her family and friends and delight in their enduring tributes to her. In these letters, we relish a lifetime of astute living learned in daily step with the Lord.

Her letters and writings supply a unique and fascinating documentary: a look into the past through family remembrance books; a plunge into the historical setting of her family and faith activities firmly rooted in the Council Bluffs, Iowa, and Omaha, Nebraska areas; a crossroads for the westward expansion of the United States and the implications of it for Evangelical and Fundamentalist Christianity; and her surprising connections to a worldwide iconic foods enterprise, Kellogg's Company.

Part biography and part memoir, Leona's example of godly living in grateful obedience to Christ is a treasure to share and a testament to the historic practice of *hesed*: sacrificial kindness and loving acts toward others in need. The latitude of her letters and life opens a world of the "extraordinary" ordinary: joy, grace, and a "kinsman redeemer" kind of love. It is a challenge to all—what if *we* lived Grandma's exemplary *hesed* today?

Leona Mae Smith Moats

REFERENCES

Marsden, George M. *Fundamentalism and American Culture.* Oxford University Press, 1980.

Hatch, Nathan O. *The Democratization of American Christianity.* Yale University Press, 1989.

Carpenter, Joel A. *Revive Us Again: The Reawakening of American Fundamentalism.* Oxford University Press, 1997.

Duguid, Iain M. *Ester & Ruth: Reformed Expository Commentary.* P&R Publishing, Phillipsburg, New Jersey, 2005.

Scripture taken from the New King James Version, *The Nelson Study Bible*, copyright © 1979, 1980, 1982, 1997 by Thomas Nelson, Inc. Used by permission. All rights reserved.

Friend, Dennis. *Old School: A Brief History of the Council Bluffs' School Buildings.* The Daily Nonpareil, July 12, 2009.

The Daily Times. *Butcher Murder Leading Event in City History.* The Missouri Valley Daily Times; Missouri Valley, Iowa. Volume 52, Number 34, Wednesday, August 16, 1939.

State Historical Society of Iowa. *Railroads in Iowa Pt. 1: How did the railroad shape the landscape of Iowa?* https://iowaculture.gov/sitesrailroadpt1-teaching guide 2019.

University of Northern Iowa; Iowa Railway Guide. *Iowa's Rail History.* http://iowahist.uni.edu/Frontier_Life/Railway_Guide2019.

Mountjoy, Eileen. *A Woman's Day: Work and Anxiety.* Indiana University of Pennsylvania. https://www.iup.edu/library/departments/archives/coal/people-lives-stories/a-womans-day-work-and-anxiety.html/©2007–2020 Indiana University of Pennsylvania.

The Coal and Coke Heritage Center. Penn State Fayette, The Eberly Campus. https://Fayette.psu.edu/visit/coalandcoke. 2020.

Stratton, Joanna L. *Pioneer Women: Voices from the Kansas Frontier.* Simon and Schuster, New York, 1981.

Mountjoy, Eileen. *Ernest: Life in a Mining Town.* Indiana University of Pennsylvania. https://iup.edu/archives/coal/people-lives-stories/ernest-life-in-a-mining-town/©2007–2020   Indiana University of Pennsylvania.

Hovanec, Evelyn A. *Common Lives of Uncommon Strength: The Women of the Coal and Coke Era of Southwestern Pennsylvania.* Pittsburgh: University of Pittsburgh Press, 1991.

Brophy, John. *A Miner's Life, An Autobiography.* Madison: University of Wisconsin Press, 1964.

Johnson, Tom. *Writing as a Holy Calling.* idratherbewriting.com; July 9. 2012.

Denny, Jim. *The Holy Calling of Writing: Are You Called to Write?* Inspire Christian Writers; inspirewriters.com. August 1, 2013.

Mathis, David. *God Made You a Writer: An Invitation to Every Christian.* desiringGod.org; August 24, 2017.

Piper, John. *Has God Called Me to Write?* desiringGod.org; June 9, 2015.

Stafford, William. *You Must Revise Your Life.* Ann Arbor: The University of Michigan Press, 1986.

Evans, John F. EdD. *Legacy Writing.* psychologytoday.com; March 9, 2014.

Sproul, R. C. *The Place of Prayer in the Christian Life.* Ligonier.org; May 3, 2014.

Bosak, Susan V. *What is legacy?* From Susan Shares: legacyproject.org/blog/February 12, 2020.

Reformed Bible Studies & Devotionals. *What is Providence?* Ligonier Ministries, Ligonier.org; April 15, 2020.

Martin, Albert. *The Journey of Faith.* Ligonier.com; *Tabletalk Magazine*, February 1, 2016.

Peterson, Jess. *A Short History of the Early Development of Omaha Nebraska.* historicomaha.com/hstrypag.htm. July 4, 2020.

usarmymodels.com/ARTICLES/Rations/krations.html.7/16/20

kellogghistory.com/timeline/html7/16/20

Battle Creek Sanitarium. En.wikipedia.org/wiki/Battle_Creek_Sanitarium. 7/5/20

Wilson, Brian C. *Dr. John Harvey Kellogg and the Religion of Biologic Living.* Indiana University Press, Bloomington, Indiana 47405. Iupress.indiana.edu 2014.

History of the Seventh-day Adventist Church. en.wikipedia.org/wiki/History_of_the_Seventh-day_Adventist_Church. July 24, 2020.

White, Arthur L. *Ellen G. White—A Brief Biography.* https: www.whiteestate.org/about/egwbio. July 24, 2020.

Mohaupt, Hillary. *Following Success with Wheat: Flaked Rice and Corn Flakes 1898.* Science History Institute: https://www.sciencehistory.org/distillations/a-recipe-for-good-health. December 30, 2019.

councilbluffs-ia.gov/2125/Our-History

historicomaha.com/hstrypag.htm. Jess Peterson; *A Short History of the Early Development of Omaha Nebraska.* 7/4/20.

usarmymodels.com/ARTICLES/Rations/krations.html. 7/17/20.

kellogghistory.com/timeline.html. 7/16/20.

battlecreektabernaclemi.adventistchurch.org. October 17, 2020.

The Art of Journaling: How to Start Journaling, Benefits of Journaling, and More. dailystoic.com/journaling; January 31, 2021.

Blanshard, Brand. *Four Reasonable Men.* Wesleyan University Press, Middleton, CT. 06459. 1984.

Powers, Bobby. *The Lost Art of Commonplacing.* Writingcooperative.com/the-lost-art-of-commonplacing. March 28, 2019.

The Nearness of God in His Word. Devotional. ligonier.org; February 9, 2021.

Grant, George. *The High Call of Service.* ligonier.org; *Tabletalk Magazine,* May 1, 2008. February 10, 2021.

Rothwell, Robert. *Why Do We Suffer?* ligonier.org; June 1, 2005; February 10, 2021.

Phillips, Richard. *A Tapestry of Faith.* ligonier.org/learn/articles/tapestry-faith. January 1st, 2004. February 10, 2021.

Campbell, Iain D. *Music in the Church.* Tabletalk Magazine, July 2010; ligonier.org/learn/devotionals/music-church/

The Music of the Covenant. February 20, 2021. ligonier.org/learn/devotionals/music-covenant/

The Beauty of Worship. February 20, 2021. igonier.org/learn/the-beauty-of-worship/

Ruark, J. Edward. *You May Have the Joy Bells.* Music by William J. Kirkpatrick. February 18, 2021. christianmusicandhymns.com.

Isaac Watts. February 18, 2021. songsandhymns.org.

Gardner, Kevin D. *Sing Like a Calvinist.* tabletalkmagazine.com/daily-study/2014/05/sing-like-a-calvinist/

Van Meggelen, Randall. *The Service of Worship.* tabletalkmagazine.com/article/2008/10/service-worship

Leckebusch, Martin. *Short Guide #1.* February 20, 2021. The Hymn Society of Great Britain & Ireland.

Holman, Colin. *Luther: The Musician.* February 20, 2021. christianitytoday.com/history/2018/march/martin-luther-musician/

Shalk, Carl. *Praising God in Song.* Concordia Publishing House, 1993. blog.cph.org; February 12. 2019.

Stewart, Rev. Angus. *The Historical Use of Psalms.* Covenant Protestant Reformed Church Northern Ireland; pastor@cprc.co.uk. February 25, 2021.

Lole, Simon. *A Brief History of Hymns.* BBC One Songs of Praise. bbc.co.uk@2021. February 25, 2021.

Lusher, Paul. *Isaac Watts.* Center for Church Music; Grand Haven, MI songsandhymns.org. February 27, 2021.

Christianity Today. *Christian History: Charles Wesley.* christianitytoday.com/history/people/poets/Charles-wesley/

Dallimore, Arnold A. *Spurgeon: A Biography.* Carlisle, PA: The Banner of Truth Trust, 1985, 2004.

Kelly, Douglas F. *Bedtime Stories.* tabletalkmagazine.com/article/2008/11/bedtime-stories/

Petersen, John. *Where is Your Treasure?* tabletalkmagazine.com/daily-study/2008/03/where-is-your-treasure/

Strachan, Owen. *The Religious Affections.* tabletalkmagazine.com/article/2012/08/the-religious-affections/

Wilson, The Rev. Jeffrey B. *Step by Step with the Lord.* Lord's Day Worship and Sermon, August 23, 2020; Providence Orthodox Presbyterian Church, Southfield, Michigan.

Rankin, W. Duncan. *Being and Becoming.* tabletalkmagazine.com/article/2010/05/being-and-becoming/.

Dumas, Dan. *The High Cost of Ambivalence.* tabletalkmagazine.com/article/2012/07/the-high-cost-of-ambivalence.

Friederichsen, Donny. *Kindness and Patience as A Witness.* tabletalkmagazine.com/article/2019/06/kindness-and-patience-as-a-witness.

What is Providence? *Devotional.* Ligonier.org; tabletalkmagazine.com/July 2007.

Beach, Dr. J. Mark. *The Blessing of God's Discipline.* tabletalkmagazine/article/2013/08/blessing-gods-discipline/

Kruger, Melissa. *Make Every Moment Count.* tabletalkmagazine.com/daily-study/2017/01/make-every-moment-count/

Wedgeworth, Steven. *Your Family is the Frontlines.* desiringgod.org/articles/your-family-is-the-frontlines/April 22, 2020.

Graham, Philip Ryken. *Hearts Aflame: Reformed Piety.* tabletalkmagazine.com/article/2005/11/hearts-aflame-reformed-piety/

Clark, R. Scott. *Reformed Piety and Practice.* tabletalkmagazine.com/article/2017/04/reformed-piety-and-practice/

Beeke, Dr. Joel R. *How Do We Glorify God?* blog post, June 3, 2017. From Living for God's Glory: An Introduction to Calvinism. Reformation Trust Publishing 2008.

Thomas, Derek. *The Christian Life as Pilgrimage.* tabletalkmagazine.com/article/2016/03/Christian-life-pilgrimage/

Di Stefano, Joseph N. *'Bible business has really gone soft': Philly printer to lay off 174, shut plant by Christmas.* The Philadelphia Inquirer; November 1, 2019.

Gutjahr, Paul C. *American History Through Literature 1820–1870: The Bible.* Encyclopedia.com/arts/culture-magazines/bible.

Bubis, Dan. *On This Day in History—September 12, 1782: Congress authorizes first printing of the Bible.* Revolutionaly-war-and-beyond.com; ©2008–2020.

Petersen, Jonathan. *History of the American Bible Society: An Interview with John Fea.* biblegateway.com; May 22, 2016.

Fortson III, Dr. S. Donald. *Overview of the Twentieth Century.* table-talkmagazine.com/article/2020/05/overview-of-the-twentieth-century/

Longhenry, Ethan. *A Study of Denominations: Historical Overview. Part II Movements.* astudyofdenominations.com.

Godfrey, W. Robert. *A Study of Church History Part 5: A.D. 1800–1900.* Ligonier Ministry Teaching Series; ligonier.org; September 15, 2015.

George Whitefield. En.wikipedia.org/wiki/George_Whitefield.

Charles Grandison Finney. Christianhistoryinstitute.org/magazine/article/Charles-grandison-finney/

Billy Sunday. Christianitytoday.com/history/people/evangelistsand apologists/billy-sunday.

Billy Graham. Billygraham.org/about/biographies/billy-graham.

Youth for Christ. yfci.org/about/history.

Dwight L. Moody. christianitytoday.com/history/people/evangelists andapologists/dwight-l-moody

D.L. Moody. Moody.edu/about/our-bold-legacy/

Evangelical History. thegospelcoalition.org/blogs/evangelical-history/historians-quietly-rewriting-typical-story-american-fundamen-talism-evangelicalism/

McIntosh, Matthew A. *A History of Evangelicalism in the United States.* brewminate.com/a-history-of-evangelicalism-in-the-united-states/

Payne, Jon. *Why Study Church History?* ligonier.org/learn/articles/why-study-church-history/

Veith, Dr. Gene Edward. *Working unto the Glory of God.* tabletalkmag-azine.com/article/2018/09/working-unto-the-glory-of-god/

A Cause to Glory in Christ Jesus. tabletalkmagazine.com/daily-study/2011/10/a-cause-to-glory-in-christ-jesus/

Riddlebarger, Dr. Kim. *The Cause and the Effect.* tabletalkmagazine.com/daily-study/2009/04/the-cause-and-the-effect/

Stallsmith, Glenn. *Worship in Meaningful Ways.* meaningfulworship.blogspot.com/2017/05/what-is-parachurch-organization

Aglow International: About Us. aglow.org/about-us/

Fourth Great Awakening. En.wikipedia.org/wiki/Fourth_Great_ Awakening

Thornton, Bill. Facebook post, March 4, 2020. Facebook.com/ pages/Dodge-Memorial-Christian-Church/

Payne, Jon. *Why Study Church History?* ligonier.org/learn/articles/ why-study-church-history/

Ellman, Lacy Clark. *10 Types of Pilgrimage—A Sacred Journey.* asa-credjourney.net/types-of-pilgrimage.

Pickowicz, Nate. *The Importance of Christian Biography.* tabletalkmaga-zine.com/posts/the-importance-of-christian-biography-2019-07/

Piper, John. *Brothers, Read Christian Biography.* desiringgod.org/arti-cles/brothers-read-christian-biography. January 1, 1995.

Cook, Faith. *Why Read Christian Biography?* banneroftruth.org. September 30, 2011.

The Messiah in History. tabletalkmagazine.com/daily-study/2019/03/ the-messiah-in-history/

Van Eyk, Stephanie. *The Ultimate Kinsman Redeemer.* ligonier.org/ blog/ultimate-kinsman-redeemer. June 5, 2013.

Trinity Hymnal, Revised Edition, Great Commission Publications, Orthodox Presbyterian Church. Presbyterian Church in America. © 1990 Great Commission Publications Inc. Suwanee, GA.

"International Sweethearts Elected for Kellogg's 50th Anniversary Celebration." Leo Burnett Company Inc., 1956. Press Release.

ABOUT THE AUTHOR

Joyce Harlukowicz is an award-winning artist, poet, and essayist living in Rochester Hills, Michigan. A graduate of Central Michigan University and Michigan State University, she served the Imlay City Community Schools for thirty-five years as a physical education and English language arts teacher. She is a member of Providence Orthodox Presbyterian Church in Southfield, Michigan.

CPSIA information can be obtained
at www.ICGtesting.com
Printed in the USA
LVHW032242261022
731684LV00016B/96